Reichian Character Structure

Structure

by Devaraj Sandberg

First Edition, 2022

The moral rights of the author have been asserted

ISBNs
978-0-9957708-6-7 (paperback)
979-8-8092169-0-6 (hardback)
978-0-9957708-5-0 (eBook)

Published by Devaraj Nick Sandberg

Illustrations by Leonie Isaacs & Victor Nassar
Cover Design by Leonie Isaacs

All enquiries to devaraj227@gmail.com
Author's Website: bioenergetics.org.uk

Contents

The Man Who Wouldn't Compromise

Wilhelm Reich

I have often noticed a tendency in human culture to simply assume that the era in which we now live is the most advanced that has ever existed. That we represent the pinnacle of all human knowledge and progress. That we stand on the shoulders of those generations that came before us. Yes, some things may have been lost to the past. But they probably didn't matter so much, otherwise someone would have picked them up.

Now, entering my sixties, I'm no longer so convinced that this is true. I think the passage of time has obscured from view some stuff that could today actually be of immense value. This book will be about one of those things – Reichian Character Structure.

Back in the 1920s, psychologist Wilhelm Reich, a student of Sigmund Freud, first began to develop the idea that our personality, body posture and the ways we coped with our childhood were all closely interlinked. He forged the notion of there being four distinct types of Character Structure, each featuring a specific type of body and certain characteristic personality traits. He unveiled his ideas in his 1933 book *Character Analysis*.

In addition to creating theories, Reich also developed ways of practically working with an individual's Character Structure as a therapist in one-to-one sessions. Asking his clients to lie down on a massage table, he would get them to breathe in a certain manner, to perform specific movements or to make certain sounds. At times, without warning, he might prod certain areas of their body with his fingers, eliciting a physical and vocal response.

Reich used these techniques to work on a client's *muscular armour* – the physical manifestation of their Character Structure. Muscular Armouring was the term he gave to areas of tension that had developed as a result of the repression of certain aspects of childhood experience. As well as tension, the concept of *armouring* included areas of the body fascia that had gone limp and lost toning, also a manifestation of their Character Structure.

The name Reich chose for his style of therapy was "Vegetotherapy," to emphasise that he was not working with the mind but rather going directly into the muscles and body fascia. Over the years, his therapeutic style came to be renamed simply "Reichian Therapy" and this is the name I will use from now on.

So, to sum up, Reich developed three ideas, all very new to the world of psychology.

Character Structure – 4 specific body types that represented both specific personality types and specific types of childhood experience.

Muscular Armouring – his name for the actual warping of the body that took place as a result of childhood influences.

Reichian Therapy – his style of working directly with the body to slowly release muscular armouring.

In addition to these new tools, when working with clients, Reich also practised conventional psychoanalysis, to assist the individual in understanding how their childhood related to their Character Structure and armouring.

The emergent world of psychology was excited by Reich's work. People sought out his books and prominent thinkers of the day discussed their implications at length. The well-to-do of early twentieth century Europe beat a path to Vienna, to be analysed and to discover which type of Character Structure they had. Reich's status as Freud's "favourite," and thus his assumed successor, was cemented firmly in the minds of his contemporaries.

It seemed for a while that Reich's notion of "Character Structure" might become a core element in the field of psychology, at that time still very much in development. As the years passed, it retained its essential appeal to the minds of new students. More insights were published regularly in books by other psychoanalysts and by Reich himself. For a period, it seemed that working with the body would become an integral element in psychology itself. But history had other ideas.

Across the Austrian border, in Germany, the rise of Adolf Hitler increasingly disturbed the fragile peace that had prevailed in Vienna and allowed psychoanalysis to flourish. Reich himself, after spending time in Germany and Norway, flirting with communism and championing sexual revolution, elected to flee to America, concerned that his interests were getting him into hot water. Both the communists and the Nazis had condemned his work, the latter actually burning his books. Arriving in New York in 1939, Reich rapidly found himself surrounded by eager new students – young Americans happy to capitalise on the flight of new and radical thinkers from Europe.

Therapy, however, was not Reich's sole interest. Although he had begun in the field of human psychology, it was not in Reich's nature to limit himself to one area. In his later years in Europe, he had sought to integrate his therapeutic work into a wider vision of how the world truly functioned, one considerably at odds with the scientific paradigm at the time.

Reich had formulated the notion of *Orgone* – a universal energy similar to Eastern ideas of *chi* or *prana*. The restriction of this energy, he hypothesised, was the root cause of all personal and societal issues. We felt rigid and unalive because Orgone was not flowing properly within us. We became attracted to fascism because the natural flow of Orgone in society was blocked.

Once established in the States, Reich returned to his studies of Orgone. He purchased microscopes and other technical machinery with which he set out to research it further. He hoped to find scientific proof of its existence and claimed some success. Reich's theory of Orgone thus became the cornerstone of his work. Character Structure and muscular armouring were merely one facet of Orgone – that relating to the body and the psyche.

As his time in the States progressed, Reich's scientific work began to take its toll on his standing in the field of psychology. It was one thing to develop novel, exciting ideas for an entirely new field. But quite another to insist that you could prove that fields of established science, such as physics or biology, had got their first principles wrong. Scientist after scientist scoffed at his theory of Orgone, piling on the ridicule, and claiming simple alternative explanations for the phenomena that he claimed to have discovered.

Early in the 1940s, Reich had succeeded in forging a connection with Albert Einstein, another escapee from war-torn Europe, who was at the time held in the highest esteem for his development of the Theory of Relativity. But, whilst initially interested, Einstein too was unconvinced of Reich's Orgone theory and would not give it credence.

For many people, finding yourself revered for your work in one field, yet ridiculed for your activities in another, it might seem reasonable to pursue the former and drop the latter. But Reich was not the type to drop a pursuit simply because he was becoming ridiculed and marginalised for it. He simply did not see the fields of hard science and human psychology as separate when it came to Orgone. He earnestly believed in a unified approach, even though this went against the grain of the more compartmentalised way that the different sciences had developed in the West.

Reich purchased land in Rangely, Maine and continued his Orgone studies there. He carried out experiments, developed theories and regularly published papers and books. Whilst it could be said that his pursuit of Orgone did little to support the reach of his psychological work to a wider audience, it also by no means entirely blocked it. Interested students still arrived at his door, seeking to learn from him. He continued to attract a wide variety of influential individuals, including novelists Saul Bellow and Norman Mailer, who would become fascinated and inspired by his theories. He attracted investment from more progressive businessmen.

However, as the 1940s drew to a close, the marginalisation of Reich unfortunately progressed to a new level. He began to attract the attention of certain American journalists, keen to make him out to be a 'quack' who was simply exploiting gullible consumers with his theory of Orgone.

Reich had developed a machine he called the Orgone Accumulator. This was simply a box, constructed of alternating layers of organic and inorganic material, in which a person could sit and experience having their orgone energy raised. Reich claimed, amongst other things, that the Accumulator could be employed to alleviate the progression of cancer. Another usage of Orgone was a machine Reich created that became known as the 'cloudbuster,' with which he claimed he could cause rain on a cloudless day.

Reich's claims were picked up, and exaggerated, in an article in Harper's magazine where they began to attract the attention of the US Government, in the form of the newly-created Food & Drug Administration – the FDA. They began to investigate Wilhelm Reich and came to the conclusion that he was indeed a fake who was making a living pushing fraudulent inventions. The FDA launched criminal proceedings against him.

Reich's continued standing as a progressive however drew him considerable legal support. Whilst many remained on the fence about Orgone, his study of Character Structure and his therapeutic style still garnered respect. A defence was mounted. Reich however could not easily bring himself to follow the advice of the legal experts who were keen to support him. Although not familiar with the US court system, he preferred to do things his way and to mount his own defence. Over many years of court appearances, this finally led to him being sentenced to two years imprisonment in a federal institution. Some months into his term, he sadly passed away from a heart condition.

Some modern-day commentators have chosen to see Reich as the victim of a high-level conspiracy to suppress alternative medical treatments. But personally, I perceive him more as a man whose strength of will was simultaneously what gave him the power to challenge existing ideas and forge new ones, and yet also finally led to his downfall. He was the man who wouldn't compromise - and all of those who have the courage to live in this manner must know inside that finally a lonely fate awaits them.

After Reich

Witnessing Reich being convicted of 'quackery,' Western psychological institutions were not slow to ensure that their own, newly forged trade did not become smeared by association. With haste, they dissociated themselves from his work, once so highly regarded. Given the direction that Western culture was developing in during this period, I think this happened with considerable ease.

By the mid-twentieth century, the power and potential of the human mind were being seen by the masses like never before. It was the development of the intellect that had furnished European and then North American culture with the capacity to forge empires and develop great wealth and power. And through the use of our rational minds, we were now creating technology that would have been unimaginable a century before. Our minds were seen as the principal tool through which our continued progress away from our humble origins as a species could advance.

In this rush to understand and develop our world through the use of the mind, inevitably the body became marginalised. To many intellectuals, the body was regarded as little more than a means to carry their minds around. I doubt it would have been difficult for those individuals at the apex of psychological institutions to conveniently drop consideration of the body in psychoanalysis. In so doing, they also relieved themselves of any need to undergo confrontational body-based process work as part of their own training!

Several of Reich's students, however, remained deeply inspired by his body-based approach to psychology, amongst them two Americans – Alexander Lowen and John Pierrakos. Both founded their own schools of therapy – Bioenergetics and Core Energetics – building upon Reich's original concepts of Character Structure and muscular armouring. In addition, other psychologists developed Reich's notion of Character Structure, simply as a useful diagnostic tool, without delving deeply into Reich's way of actually working directly with client's bodies.

In this book, I am seeking to continue this process of advancing Reich's original work on Character Structure. Not only by bringing it firmly into the twenty-first century and presenting it in a format that should be easy for anyone to grasp, but also by reintroducing both Reichian and Bioenergetic exercises for the Character Types.

The Four Original Character Types... plus one!

Reich's original book *Character Analysis*, first published in 1933, identified four fundamental Character Types. To each, he gave a name drawn from the psychoanalytic language of the time. Each also had an associated body-type and personality type. Each of these Character Types was furthermore associated with specific childhood circumstances.

For example, people with a brittle, skinny and somewhat angular physique would be characterised, in Reich's system, as *Schizoid*. At the level of their personality, they would tend to live in a rather cerebral, abstract world, their life dominated by a sense of fear, of which they were barely conscious. Invariably, this related to a feeling of not being safe in their womb environment, or in early infancy.

Secondly, there was the *Oral* type. Characteristic of this structure was a deflated chest, a malnourished look and a tendency to please. Oral Characters tend to obsess over connection and nourishment. They lack a healthy level of assertiveness and frequently believe that, no matter what happens, they will never get enough. This pattern has its origins in a lack of connection to the mother in the first year of infancy.

Another type Reich designated was the *Masochist*. This Character Type was usually heavy-set and slow to move or respond. At a personality level, they were compliant and submissive but would live life grudgingly, frequently blaming and complaining. Their inner world was invariably dominated by conflict and angst, rather as though two people were living inside of their head, constantly at odds. This pattern had its origin in being overwhelmed by a parent during the beginning of ego development, around the age of two or three years.

Finally, Reich identified the *Rigid* type. This Character would have more drive and ego development than the other three. They could be distinguished by their high level of upper body development, unmoving facial expression and set jaw. Rigid types are dominated by a need to chase goals and to move up social hierarchies. They see life as a battle that they must win, constantly preparing themselves to face opposition. Emotions are regarded as signs of personal weakness. Hence they rigidify their body and psyche to protect themselves from feelings. The roots of this type of Character lie in the later years of early childhood. They learned from their parents that rewards and love only came on condition of correct behaviour, that what matters above all in life is to function well.

Some years after Reich's original designations, a fifth Character Type was added, that of the *Psychopath*. I'm not sure of the origins of this type but it has been widely accepted. An issue with this Character Type is that it is also a designation used in modern psychiatry for a somewhat, though not altogether, different type of personality.

The *psychopath*, as understood in the field of Character Structure, typically has tight hips, a strongly developed chest and a striking face. Like the Rigid type, they also see life as a challenge that needs to be confronted. But, instead of rigidifying their body and mind, they instead have learned to channel their repressed emotional energy up their body to their face and chest. They create a powerful and charismatic front with which to face and dominate the world. They can be fluid and chameleon-like depending on the situation that faces them – sometimes overpowering, sometimes charismatic or seductive. At some point in their childhood, they usually experienced a severe loss of trust in one or both parents. As a response, they resolved to never trust anyone to such a degree again and became self-reliant, seeking to dominate the world as a form of payback.

Systems of Personality Classification

That was a basic rundown of the five Reichian Character Structures. We will be going more deeply into each of them later on. Firstly, I want to explain why this system is radically different from other ways of classifying personality types.

Over the years, many different ways of usefully putting people into different boxes have arisen. I will list a few:

- Astrology

- The Chinese Horoscope

- The Enneagram

- Myers-Briggs

- DISC Profiling

People have found these systems useful for understanding themselves better, for choosing suitable partners and finding their perfect role in an organisation. Some of these systems are ancient. Some are modern. Some are from alternative culture. Some are corporate. But all share one common attribute…

You get put in a box and you have to make the best of it!

This is not a bad thing. Having a rationale for why we are the way we are can be very useful. Knowing that I'm a Capricorn, I can more easily accept why I can be business-like and at times rigid, even when it is not appropriate. Understanding that my Myers-Briggs designation is 'Campaigner' helps me to relax with the side of me that loves to bang the drum for some particular cause, often to the annoyance of those around me. Recognising that we have a specific type of personality can bring us to a state of self-acceptance.

However, what's so unique about Reich's system of classification is that it also points us back to the specific circumstances of our childhood and indicates therapeutic work that we can do to change things.

Being designated an 'Oral Character' does not mean that I am condemned to live my life forever longing for more connection and secretly believing I will never get enough. I don't just need to learn to 'work around' these traits. It's not a life sentence. There are exercises that I can do, and behaviours that I can learn, to overcome the negative or limiting aspects of this type and restore myself to a state of inner harmony.

This is the case for all of these five Character Types. They are not simply labels. They are signposts that function on multiple levels to show us how many of our different aspects are actually tied together. The way we coped with our specific childhood relates both to how our personality and our body developed as we came into adulthood.

How This Book Works

As I mentioned earlier on, my aim in this book is not only to provide up-to-date, purposeful information about these Character Types but also to give both physical and mental exercises that can help us overcome their negative aspects.

I will devote one chapter to each of the 5 Character Types, followed by a chapter about combinations. Each chapter will begin by describing the Character Type in detail, looking at elements of the personality, inner world and physical development, and the childhood dynamic that creates it. I will include the positive aspects of each Character Type as well as the limiting aspects. I will give a classification of how open, grounded and assertive that type is – three qualities that I will explain in more detail shortly.

Then I will give a list of Bioenergetic and Reichian exercises that can be employed over time to progressively relieve us of the more limiting aspects of that Character Type. As we both understand and work on these traits within ourselves, so we heal the past and can step forwards beyond the limitations that our childhood environment embodied in us. This book is intended as a complete, standalone guide to both understanding and working with the life-limiting aspects of Character Structure.

Throughout this book, I am capitalising the first letters of words and phrases like the following:

- Character Structure

- Character Type

- Pattern

- Strategy

This is to indicate when their usage is strictly in the context of Character Analysis and so to help alleviate any confusion.

Principles

The Sense of the Body

For most of us, the sense of our body is not an exciting thing. Not compared to our thinking, our emotions and our sensory experiences. But that is just because our bodies have become 'shut down.' They have lost their natural vibrant aliveness. We have come to dismiss our sense of the body but actually it should be the cornerstone of our awareness. This has happened for precisely the reasons that we looked at in the last chapter - the repression of feelings associated with aspects of our early childhood experience.

In addition, because we tend to favour thinking over feeling the sense of the body, we often develop thinking behaviours that provide us with adequate pleasure to function well. Our dopamine systems become calibrated for specific, thought-based behaviours that we repetitively need to undertake in order to get a 'thrill' from life. These addictive tendencies would not be needed if we could feel our bodies more. The sense of the body, when it is not crammed full of repressed energy and emotionality, will provide us with more than enough energy and sense of thrill, simply through being alive.

So, a big part of the exercise section of this book will be aimed at getting the repression out and allowing our body to give us all the energy, love and excitement we need in a natural way.

Grounding, Assertiveness & Openness

Working as a therapist for many years, in a field that has grown some-what out of fashion, I have found it useful to develop a few of my own terms and concepts, to bring things up-to-date and to make ideas more accessible. One of these is the notion of three energetic channels in the psyche that we can usefully open.

The idea of 'somatic centres' in the body or psyche is one of those con-cepts that can be very useful. Even though we don't know how scien-tifically valid such an idea is, it is nevertheless popular colloquially. We may often experience ourselves as "blocked at the throat" when we fail to speak up in a situation where we actually needed to. Or we may feel that our "heart is closed" when we cannot access our deeper feelings or vulnerability. Perhaps, we sometimes feel "stuck in the head" – unable to stop thinking and suspecting that we're avoiding emotions under the surface.

I myself make use of the notion of somatic centres when teaching. But what I have found to be even more useful, as well as more simple, is the notion that there exist three channels. These are:

1) The Grounding Channel – from the belly to the soles of the feet.

2) The Assertiveness Channel – from the belly to the throat.

3) The Heart Channel – from the heart to the head.

To me, these channels are not just concepts. I can actually sense them in my experience of the body. As a therapist, I work with clients to support them to get these three channels open. Because, if they can do that – they won't need therapy any more!

Most people, in my experience, have all three mostly closed. Some may have one open. I will briefly go through these three channels, explaining a little more what they're about. This is relevant because, when we get to the Character Structures themselves, I will correlate each type to how open or closed each of these channels usually are.

The Grounding Channel

You are likely familiar with the term *grounded*. It infers that a person has his or her feet on the ground. It means that they are solid, dependable and not likely to fly off into fantasies. Becoming grounded means actually opening up this channel in our psyche. It means getting more feeling in our belly, so that we can sense its volatile, fiery energy. It also means clearing out any energetic or muscular blocks between our belly and the soles of our feet. This latter means working with the pelvis and the legs. Perhaps our psoas muscles have a lot of holding patterns in them, or our calves. *Holding patterns* are what we call areas of unnatural rigidity and tension in our muscles or body fascia. This *holding* represents a charge of energy that is held in these muscles and thus does not flow freely. We can use specific Reichian or Bioenergetic exercises to release this holding and then we will feel more grounded, more connected to the earth.

The Assertiveness Channel

As mentioned above, it's very useful to develop more energy and feeling in our belly. Many people these days have an inadequate sense of the belly in their day-to-day experience. Without the presence of this sense of the belly, our life is inevitably more mechanistic, more defined by thinking, and lacking animal intensity and passion. The circuit of the body we're looking at here runs again from the belly, but this time up the body to the throat. When this circuit is open we feel okay to both feel and express our animal intensity. It gives us passion and charisma. It also enables us to naturally express our boundaries.

When our throat is closed, we might feel a lot inside, but we will not express it. We will keep everything pushed down. The result is a recipe for depression. Having this belly-throat channel open, not only do we feel vibrantly alive, but we can transmit this feeling to the world around us. We are naturally and immediately responsive to life, no longer needing to think everything through five times before acting. People can sense in us that we are in the moment, unafraid of life.

The Heart Channel

Very few people have any of these channels properly open. But say that we did meet someone who does have the above two open. They are grounded and they are filled with dynamic responsiveness and charisma. If we met such a person, we might feel initially overawed. But perhaps after a while we would notice that something was still missing from within them – the heart connection. This is a sense of natural openness and a willingness to allow vulnerability. If we say that our heart is open then we mean that we are in a state of trust with another and are not protecting our inner world through judgments. I consider this to be a circuit that runs from our energetic heart, in the centre of our chest, to our brain, or our mind.

I say 'energetic heart' because usually this centre is felt not in the physical heart, aligned slightly to the left, but rather in the middle of the chest. If you have ever wept with deep grief over something that happened, it may have felt like a dam bursting open in the middle of your chest.

With our Heart Channel open, now we are no longer afraid of vulnerability. We seek out depth in our relating to others and naturally desire to surround ourselves with others who are okay with allowing vulnerability.

But, of itself, the Heart Channel is very limited if the other two circuits remain closed. Having spent a chunk of my life living communally and in spiritual communities, I have met many with solely this channel open. Whilst they are often beautiful people, they do struggle to be in the world and have to seek out specific environments in order to feel safe. As a human, the goal is to open all three channels.

Do We Only Have One Character Type?

When the notion of Character Structure was first articulated by Reich, and throughout its continued development, one concept remained the same. You have one primary and one secondary Character Type. The primary is your main Type. When I first came across the concept of Character Structure, whilst training to be a therapist in the early 2000s, I was diagnosed 'Oral' as a primary and 'Rigid' as a secondary. I would consider this accurate and I can certainly still see the residue of those characters in my personality today.

However, when I began to work more deeply with Character Structure, some fifteen years later, it became clear to me that, in fact, I had all five Character Types within me. Coming to understand how each of them operated on a deeper level, I could absolutely see myself responding to different situations in these different ways.

Around new, scary situations I became Aggressive or Rigid. In love relationships, I could be strongly Oral though with different modes of covering up or compensating for this. In work situations, my default was Aggressive until I felt I had to wind it down a bit and listen more. I could also see strong Endurer traits in work – at times not really making the most of what I had but just plodding along in a state of low self-esteem. In friendships, I could be quite Aggressive until I sensed a deeper sense of trust arising between myself and the person. When on my own, my default was actually more to dissociate – what we will come to term 'Leaving.'

In addition to what I saw in myself, now that I was creating more and more content about Character Structure, including a popular online quiz where you could work yours out, many people were reporting similar results. They could also see all 5 Character Types living within them.

How to make sense of this? What I elected to do was to present Character Structure as a series of five 'Safety Strategies' which our developing psyche had access to. This term was first coined by therapist Steven Kessler. One of these safety strategies would be invoked by our brain whenever we encountered a situation that we couldn't process emotionally in the moment. Over time, if we kept on invoking this same strategy, slowly it would become an aspect of both our personality and our physical appearance. Thus, the individual would have access to all these strategies but several would probably become more dominant over time, as they were repeatedly invoked.

We will look more practically at 'safety strategies' in a moment. But for now it's enough to understand that, whilst all of these strategies exist within us, there is likely to be one that is dominant and one that is secondary. So, it's good to work initially on these, though this in no way precludes you from working on the others as well.

Before moving on, I want to mention one pitfall that can occur should we consider that we have all 5 Character Types.

To overcome the limiting effects of these strategies within our own being, we have to work in an intelligent fashion over a considerable length of time. We will need a basic level of discipline. This is because, once the strategies are written deeply into both our body and mind, they will not easily dissipate. Like all mental states, they tend to have a life of their own when it comes to maintaining themselves. Our mind will repeatedly find ways to get us back into the pattern – unconsciously seeking out specific types of drama or through keeping us engaged mentally with the same old conflicts.

The belief that we have all 5 of these Character Types can easily become an excuse not to focus adequately hard on any one of them to create real change.

The Names of the Character Structures

When Wilhelm Reich first published 'Character Analysis,' back in the early 30s, it was intended solely for an audience of professional psychologists. Thus, in labelling the 4 different Character Types, he chose names that he considered fitting – Schizoid, Oral, Masochist and Rigid. Later on, as mentioned, a fifth Type was also categorised and this was named "Psychopath."

As psychology developed over the years and became more mainstream, these terms were increasingly regarded as 'pathologizing.' Understandably, few people wanted to be labelled 'masochist' or 'psychopath.' These heavy, psychiatric terms did little to encourage clients to get on board with working on their issues.

Thus, from around the 1950s onwards, different therapists introduced alternative names for these 5 Types. Each attempted to 'soften' the emotional impact of being characterised as this Type, whilst still trying to retain the essence of the original meaning.

I will not go into all the different names that have been used over the years. That would be beyond the scope of this book and not so much practical use. I will simply list below the terms that I will be using, putting the originals in brackets.

Leaving - (Schizoid)

Oral - (Oral)

Endurer - (Masochist)

Rigid - (Rigid)

Aggressive - (Psychopath)

As you can see, I have not elected to change each of the names as I don't consider "Oral" or "Rigid" to be excessively pathologizing.

Safety Strategies

In the last section, I used the term 'safety strategies.' But what does it really mean?

As infants and small children, the resources we have to deal with adverse or unexpected events are limited. Our genes have primed us to expect certain conditions to be present during our time in the womb and throughout infancy. Specifically, our brain expects the following to happen:

1) that we will feel safe and secure whilst inside our mother

2) that we will feel a strong physical and emotional bond with her for our first year

3) that our need for self-expression from the age of two, however annoying, will be tolerated by our parents, with simple, clear boundaries applied

If any of these three conditions are not met, it will likely not be possible for us to integrate the deviation from what our brain expected. To deal with this eventuality, we evolved a means of coping. Our brain engages a defensive mode of behaviour that both represses the energy and feeling arising from the unexpected situation and adapts our behaviour to create a sense of safety.

If, for example, our developing nervous system registers a feeling of "unsafety" in our womb environment, it will reduce our ability to feel our body and instead keep our attention in our developing neocortex – what will become our thinking mind.

If our brain registers that our mother is inadequately present for us, physically or emotionally, during the first year of our life, it will retain this sense of there being a lack. We will tend to look out on the world with longing, subtly or overtly seeking some other figure who will come along and give us the love or attention that we didn't get as an infant.

If we felt harshly "shut down" by our parents during our initial attempts at self-expression as a two-year old, then we will retreat inside of ourselves and learn compliant behaviours. We grow up believing that it is too dangerous to be ourselves and that submission to authority is a necessity for survival.

These three types of safety strategy correspond to the first three Character Structures – Leaving, Oral and Endurer. It can be useful to refer to these as "pre-egoic." This is because they took place before our ego – our sense of personal selfhood – began to properly form. These types of safety strategy are thus the most debilitating because they happen at the earliest phases of our life.

There are two other safety strategies that we need to consider – Rigid and Aggressive. These two are usefully labelled 'post-egoic' or simply 'egoic,' because they happen once our ego has at least begun to develop. They are thus less debilitating, though nevertheless capable of severely limiting the quality of our life.

The Rigid Character Type is the result of excessive parental conditioning from the age of around 4 onwards. If, as kids, we were taught that in order to receive love we had to behave in a way deemed 'good,' and that 'bad' behaviour would always be punished, we will be susceptible to becoming this type. We may learn to 'play by the rules' of life, focussing on how we function and rejecting how we actually feel. We learn to hold our bodies tight in an attempt to control excessive feelings. We become acutely aware of our 'status' – our place in the various social hierarchies that surround us – and seek to move up through our choice of partner, job, friendships and by developing wealth.

Finally, the Aggressive Character Type, if it comes, will tend to emerge from around the age of 6 onwards. It is usually the result of feeling deeply let down by a parent, or by another adult whom we had formerly looked up to. Perhaps we came to believe that our mother never really loved us, merely using us as a pawn in her own battle with her partner. Perhaps we came to see that our father only wanted us to get good grades to make himself look good. Whatever the situation, the feeling of being used or let down causes us to internally resolve to never deeply trust another human being again. Instead of rigidifying over our feelings, we learn to channel our emotional energy up our body and into our face and chest, creating a powerful front with which to face the world. We become charismatic and powerful. We have a certain fluidity in how we are and can adjust our personality to suit the situation we find ourselves in, such that we get what we want from it.

Thus we can see that these 5 safety strategies, each the result of situations we couldn't process in specific phases of our development, serve to define our personality on many levels. They are the roots of our Character Structure.

Leaving Characters tend to retreat into abstract thinking whenever their nervous system registers a feeling of unsafety. Oral characters forever seek some form of connection to take away the sense of emptiness that follows them around. Endurers are resigned to life and seek only to get through the day and survive, whilst their inner world remains filled with conflict and angst. Rigid characters set their jaw firmly against a hostile world and seek to fight their way to the top. Aggressives ruthlessly seek power, to pay back for the slights they suffered as children.

Our innate desire to survive and feel safe as kids is what comes to define many core aspects of our personality.

How Reich and later Therapists worked on Character Structure

Okay, so we've looked at Character Structure and the various Types. We've considered Safety Strategies, the origins of Character Structure. Now let's take a look at how therapists like Reich and those who followed in his wake actually worked on clients.

We will look first at Reichian Therapy – the source of the Reichian exercises in this book. Then at Bioenergetics, the development that Alexander Lowen and others created.

Reichian Therapy was developed for working with clients one-to-one, as opposed to working with whole groups at a time, or as a means for clients to work on themselves. Before beginning actual work on their body, the therapist would ask the client about their childhood and what they recalled of their relationship with their parents, as is normal in psychotherapy. He or she would also observe them as they moved about the room, taking in their body language and habitual posture. From these observations, the therapist would make a preliminary diagnosis of their Character Structure.

Then the work could begin. The therapist would ask the client to get onto the massage table and direct them to lie on their back with their knees up and eyes open – a position known as the 'Reichian Working Position.' Invariably, he or she worked with clients in their underwear so that he could observe their muscles and body fascia.

The therapist would then direct the person to breathe or to move in a certain way or perhaps to make sound. He or she might have them bash their fists down on a cushion whilst making as loud a sound as they could muster. At times, and often unexpectedly, the therapist would prod certain muscles – perhaps the epigastrium – to deliberately provoke a reaction and then direct the client to express the feeling that came up.

The underlying direction of Reichian Therapy was to take clients out of the 'comfort zone' that they had built up around themselves. From the situations of their childhoods, clients had closed themselves off to their full human potential and were existing as pale substitutes of their true selves. By invoking powerful and provocative emotional experiences within them - through having them move, make sound and also by prodding them - the therapist activated their egoic defences and encouraged them to express what was repressed, rather than attempt to hold it in.

In this manner, over a course of months or years, clients gradually broke through the boundaries they had set around their innate emotionality and behaviour. They began to feel truly alive.

Prior to Reich, therapy had consisted almost solely of psychoanalysis. Freud would get clients to lie semi-prone on a chaise longue whilst he asked them about their dreams, their unfulfilled aspirations, or their relationship with their parents. The psychoanalyst invariably remained out of sight of the client during the session. Thus, Reich's work was truly radical and exciting. Not because he dropped psychoanalysis, far from it. But because he augmented it with body analysis and bodywork.

From the time he arrived in the States, Reich attracted many therapists or therapists-in-training to his work. People wanted to get involved. They wanted to learn from him, so they could augment their own practice with what he had developed. Reich insisted on two things from potential trainees. Firstly, they had to have graduated as doctors of medicine. Secondly, they must first undergo Reichian Therapy themselves.

One of Reich's students was Alexander Lowen. When he completed his training with Reich, he began to take the work in a new direction. Lowen developed what he came to call 'Bioenergetics.'

Bioenergetics differed from Reichian Therapy in that Lowen introduced more postures to be done standing up and kneeling, as well as those done lying on a mattress. He added still more expression exercises, getting clients to put out their inner angst and rage through bashing pillows or whacking a knotted towel against the floor whilst screaming. He also introduced static standing postures, where the focus was to try to maintain and deepen the posture whilst breathing from the belly.

Like Reich before him, Lowen continued to utilise these physical exercises as an adjunct to psychoanalysis. His clients continued to have to relate what was going on in their life and speak of their childhoods. However, one big difference with Lowen's Bioenergetics, was that it was no longer so necessary for the therapist to stand over the client, or to push or prod him or her. Now he could direct things from a little way away. This opened the doorway to therapists giving clients exercises that they could work with when alone, in between sessions.

Fifty years down the line, it is nowadays easier than ever for interested people to make a reasonable degree of progress working by themselves with these techniques, assuming they have good discipline and an understanding of Character Structure. Whilst we will always have blind spots – making work with a therapist very useful – we can nevertheless overcome a lot of our issues through self-honesty, discipline, theoretical understanding, and physical therapeutic work. This is what this book is about – giving you the understanding and the techniques. What you will have to bring is self-honesty and discipline.

The Goal of Therapy – Grounding and Openness

How will we know when we are fixed? This question, not unreasonably, occupies many of those who come to work on themselves. The answer is… when we can get our needs met authentically and have a life we feel proud of.

So, do our issues just go away if we do enough therapy? Actually, no. The human psyche appears to be layered, rather like an onion. Clearing a personal issue out on one level may cause it to disappear for a while, only to inevitably return on a deeper level later! This seems like bad news. But it is just the way things are. What is different about working with the body in therapy is that you progressively release the charge of energy held within the musculature and fascia. It is this charge, along with our negative beliefs and behaviours, that create our life problems.

In traditional psychotherapy, we look at the behaviours that we have that are causing issues in our lives – perhaps repeatedly getting into relationships with the "wrong kind" of partners; perhaps always putting our own needs second. The therapist then guides us to make connections with the events of our childhood, maybe freeing up some repressed feelings within us, and encourages us to develop more healthy behaviours.

What is missing in this otherwise excellent process is a connection to the body. Because it is the body where the bulk of the repressed charge is stored, or stuck. Likewise, it is the body, and especially the area of the throat, neck and shoulders, where maladaptive breathing is constantly maintaining self-restricting holding patterns. The net result of these factors is to constantly drag you back into negative behaviours because the energy held there has not been released.

We might, for example, elect to change our negative self-image of being an 'unworthy, incapable person' into that of someone who 'can do it and who deserves an excellent life.' This is great and may provide a sense of renewal and transformation for a while. But, if all the energy stuck in the body from the years when we were in the negative self-belief is not released, it will pull us back into negativity again and again. It is this factor that invariably hijacks change for those who work only with therapy for the mind – your thinking patterns and your beliefs.

When we work with the Reichian and Bioenergetic exercises explained in this book, over time, we can truly release the past at a physical level.

Then, when we adopt a more positive image of who we are and what we can achieve in life, that image will stick. For there is no longer anything remaining in the body to hijack our self-transformation.

The two primary qualities that this type of therapeutic approach will give you are increased grounding and increased openness. When something triggers you, and formerly you would have flown off into an abstract world in your mind, now you will find that you can simply remain present with what is going on, maintaining safe boundaries for yourself when needed. When nothing is triggering you, you will feel more open to life – more able to simply be in the moment without needing to judge whatever is going on, or label or pigeonhole things.

This is a state that can't help but make you feel progressively better and better about your life. The more that we use judgement to create for ourselves a feeling of safety, the more that we inevitably end up judging ourselves in a negative way. As we feel more present in our bodies and more grounded, a natural sense of boundaries comes in. We no longer have to rely on learned, mental techniques to feel safe.

In addition, as we progressively release the charge of repressed energy from our system, we naturally begin to see better ways to deal with the situations that occur in our lives.

For example, someone who was heavily put down and controlled as a child will have stored within them a huge charge of repressed anger. But around that charge will likely have developed a layer of fear. To ensure that they don't feel this anger, their psyche will have learned to constantly assess who they need to be in any given situation in order to not provoke any form of confrontation. They will have become a 'pleaser.'

So, as soon as their mind spots any possibility that a situation might become confrontational, they begin to take evasive action. They change their tone. They change their opinions about a topic. They depart the scene or find something else to do. Whatever it takes. They don't even consider that they might be able to stand their ground and simply assert a clear position for themselves. Whilst the charge of energy remains repressed in their system, their behaviour is simply 'hard-wired' to avoid confrontation at all costs.

But, when a big portion of that repressed charge has been released through Reichian or Bioenergetic work, suddenly, as if by magic, new possibilities will begin to occur to them. Seeing the possibility of confrontation, perhaps they again start to take evasive action internally. But then a voice pops up on the inside saying "Why don't you just clearly state that this is not okay for you? It doesn't have to be a big confrontation." In this manner, previously suppressed possibilities now arise.

For those people who have learned to always confront, in order to control a situation, and to never, ever show vulnerability, new possibilities will also manifest. As the repressed charge associated with emotional pain that is stored within their body begins to be released, they find that, instead of having to go on the attack, now they can simply share how they actually feel and allow themselves to be vulnerable.

This is the goal of this therapeutic approach – an increased openness and grounding that results in less fear of taking a position or being vulnerable.

Coming Out of a Pre-Egoic Structure

This is perhaps a good point at which to mention a bizarre and sometimes disturbing aspect of working with the 3 'pre-egoic' Character Structures – Leaving, Oral or Enduring. As the pattern you're working on begins to dissolve, what is quite frequently seen is the sudden onset of Rigid or Aggressive Structures.

As work progresses on the pre-egoic Structure, the individual begins to experience a great deal more egoic drive and a sense of greater freedom. Being unused to this experience, and inevitably finding it somewhat disturbing, the individual will often adopt an egoic Safety Strategy, either Rigid or Aggressive.

Adopting a Rigid Structure allows some control over the strange experience they are undergoing. They can hold their new-found levels of energy in, as well as the freedom that they are now experiencing in their belief system. This gives them a reassuring sense of control, and, to a degree, this is natural and of benefit.

Adopting an Aggressive Structure allows their new energy and self-image to expand more. However, it may take the form of a strong impulse for 'payback' against the world that they perceive as having formerly repressed them.

Someone formerly dominated by the Leaving Structure, for example, as this Pattern begins to dissipate, may well experience the world, or specific individuals, as having rejected their ideas. Actually, they were simply in too much fear, when dominated by the Structure, to move forwards. But this is frequently not recognised. Filled with righteous anger, they may react aggressively to anyone they perceive as not immediately recognising their talents.

Someone formerly in the grip of the Oral Structure may likewise begin to believe that those they used to 'please,' in order to maintain the connection, were actually manipulating them or otherwise using them in some way. Filled once again with righteous anger, they may well seek payback against them in some manner.

It is those formerly strong in the Enduring Structure who require the most observation and guidance. Endurers always have huge levels of repressed anger and, as this comes to the surface, their psyche will inevitably seek 'targets' to project their new-found rage onto. Bearing in mind that many Endurers are large males, whose musculature has developed to repress their anger, it becomes clear that this could potentially be a problem. The worm has turned and may now be seeking payback.

So, whether you're working on clients or working on yourself, it's good to be attentive to this issue. As a therapist, you have a responsibility to ensure that those people around the client, and the world at large, are safe. You want to dissolve that Structure but you must also take responsibility for your work.

So be attentive to how the client is doing in the outside world if you are regularly working with them. Check in and get answers. Are they noting any increased level of anger or reactivity in their social interactions? This is especially important with people of the Enduring Type.

If issues are arising, give clear behavioural boundaries to the client. Do your best not to put them down or put them back in the 'box' from which you've just helped them to escape. But do create clear boundaries and be willing to 'wind down' the intensity of the work if you are at all concerned. You need to take responsibility.

Likewise, if you're working on your own Character Structure, practice self-awareness. It may be useful to score and keep a record of your daily or weekly anger or reactivity levels. Score yourself from 1-10 on work situations, social situations, and love relationships. Be accurate with yourself. Perhaps you are justifying your new found level of anger as fully appropriate to the situation. But are you sure you are not simply in the 'self-righteous anger' phase?

Let's spend a few paragraphs understanding the different therapeutic situations in which issues of this nature are more or less likely to occur.

Generally, when working on yourself, you are less likely to become overwhelmed with rising anger. This is because your brain's natural defences will stop your process before you get to that level. In fact, most people working in this way will need the guidance of someone experienced at some point just to keep them moving through this defensive resistance. Generally speaking, the only people at risk from this issue would be those with a history of mental health issues.

Nevertheless, be attentive, especially if you know you have a significant Endurer component to your personality. That rage will be there beneath the surface somewhere.

Working one-to-one with clients, likewise it is generally safe, for as a therapist you are fully present with one individual and can monitor how they are doing. It's important to check in each session about any background anger and reactivity that the client may be experiencing in their day-to-day life.

The main area of risk with this issue is when running groups. As group leaders, we do our best to monitor how each participant is doing. But we, and any staff we have, are limited. Thus, a good rule of thumb is to only move the group at the rate of the individual you perceive as struggling the most. Or, if this is not practicable, to keep an extra eye on this individual.

In groups, once again, it is those high in the Endurer Structure that we need to keep an eye on. In a group process, the collective energy is higher, and this can be put to good use to move people deeper. But it can also result in an individual opening up more than they can comfortably process, with ramifications especially after the workshop is finished.

As well as needing to be on the lookout for rising anger, subliminally mediated defensive reactions can equally be an issue.

Yes, some people find themselves angrier and more filled with a seemingly righteous rage towards those they believe to have oppressed them. But, equally, those with dissociating tendencies, may not get to experience the anger; rather, they just enter a state that is quite strongly dissociated from the body. In extreme situations, this can lead to psychosis or psychotic episodes, which are obviously things we wish to avoid. See the Additional Writings chapter at the end of this book for an article about this phenomenon, how to avoid it and what to do.

If you are just starting out as a group therapist, do not lose heart at the words above. Remember not to push too hard, until you are sure that you really feel where your group is at. Watch out for any desire to 'prove yourself' by leading participants into the most evocative sessions you know. Remember that you are also responsible for how your participants are after the workshop has been completed and they are back in their day-to-day lives.

Practicalities

How to use the Bioenergetic and Reichian exercises in this Book

Each of the subsequent chapters will be about a specific Character Structure, or combination of Character Structures. After giving all sorts of exciting and useful information about the Structure, there will be a list of Bioenergetic and Reichian exercises that can be employed to remove the charge of stuck energy associated with this Structure from the body. I want to write a little more about these exercises.

In the last chapters, we looked at how Reichian Therapy and Bioenergetics developed. The exercises in this book will be mostly drawn from these two fields, specifically those which are effective practices to do on one's own. We will be utilising two styles of exercises from each of these two fields:

1) **Breathing exercises from Reichian Therapy** – these are styles of actual breathing, usually practised lying down in a specific position.

2) **Armour Release exercises from Reichian Therapy** – these are exercises where you tense specific muscles, whilst breathing in one of the ways above, again usually practised lying down in a specific position.

3) Static Postures from Bioenergetics – these are exercises, usually done standing up, where you maintain a specific posture whilst breathing and feeling your body.

4) Dynamic Postures from Bioenergetics – these are repetitive movement exercises that are usually done standing up, whilst feeling your body.

Okay, so these are the four broad styles of exercise that you will find in this book. In addition, there are a few 'wild cards' – other, usually more passive exercises that I've included too.

However, simply being given therapeutic exercises like these, does not create so much change in and of itself. The way that we do each exercise - our attitude and our approach - are very important. Most of us will be used to doing exercises of some type. Perhaps we work out or we do yoga. But when we're doing exercises from body-based therapy, the approach that we take makes a huge difference.

Before getting right to the core of this, let's spend a few paragraphs looking a little at attitude and why certain exercises are good for many different Character Structures.

Perhaps in an ideal world, exercises would be specific for each Character Structure and they could be deployed to quickly release the charge of energy repressed into the body associated with that Structure. However, we do not live in such a world. Our body is way too complex and chaotic to allow itself to be so strictly compartmentalised. Some exercises will be invaluable for any of the Character Structures. Others will be more specific to one or a few. But what is common to all these exercises is that you will have to employ them with discipline and patience.

If you have come to this book hoping for a 'quick fix' for your personality, then this may not be the place for you. There is nothing wrong with seeking quick fixes. In fact, our brain's dopamine circuits are configured specifically to seek them out – something marketing gurus frequently make use of. The trouble is, when you're dealing with your body and your psychology – they don't work. There are no quick fixes. The only way you are going to get the system of bodywork revealed in these pages to work is with diligence and discipline.

You have to work with each specific exercise until you really have it 'down' inside of you. Your body itself has to 'get' the exercise, so that when you perform it you can actually feel the release happening from the inside. This will take a period of some time with each exercise. You will have to continue when your mind is thinking of myriad reasons not to. In fact, the more it doesn't want to, the more benefit you will get from continuing. In short, you will need some level of discipline.

In my two books on Bioenergetics (2020 & 2021), I go into the reasons why we experience so much resistance, especially when we are actually close to the point of change. I won't repeat myself here. I will simply say that you really need to work these exercises. Work the breath, work the body, work the sense of feeling.

When you come to the Exercises section of the chapter on a specific Character Structure, choose just one of the ten workouts listed that feels like it would be good for you to start with. It needn't be the first one listed. Then, once you have chosen one, complete it at least 14 times on separate days before moving on to another.

Okay, now we can get right to the guts of how these therapies work.

Stretch, Breathe, Feel

I could write heaps of theory about this style of therapy. But I'm not going to. It's not so necessary. In any body-based therapeutic approach, the theory is mostly just there to give the mind some understanding and some reason as to why we need to do these postures and workouts. It's main function is actually to reassure us that, yes, we really do need to keep doing this stuff in order to heal and improve. Once someone is ready to just jump in, then there's not so much need for theory.

A few paragraphs back, we listed the four main types of exercise that are found in this book. Of those four, the Bioenergetics Static Postures and the Reichian Armour Release exercises revolve around these three principles:

- Stretch

- Breathe

- Feel

We put the body into specific postures, or we tense specific muscle groups. Then we endeavour to maintain or deepen the stretch whilst breathing with the belly and feeling the body. It might sound straightforward but watch out!

The real trick is to be able to give equal attention to stretching, breathing and feeling. Many people over-focus on the posture, stretch their body like crazy, but forget all about their breathing and totally neglect to stay present with the feeling of the body. Sometimes they write me emails asking, "Can I increase the Bow posture to 15 minutes?" They are pushing the posture to the max but at the expense of the other elements. It's okay, but they would get a lot more from doing that posture for 60 seconds but really breathing and feeling.

The breathing technique for Bioenergetics we will look at in a moment, as it's actually pretty radical and needs its own little section. But I cannot emphasise enough just how important it is to keep feeling the body. We check our posture. We check our breathing. But then the rest of our awareness remains tuned in to the sense of the body.

The Reichian Breathing exercises do not involve stretching certain muscle groups. So what is important is to focus on doing the exercise right whilst remaining feeling your body.

With the Bioenergetics Dynamic Postures, paying attention to the breath is not so important because the postures are usually quite intense and it is okay to focus solely on completing the exercise and feeling the body.

What you will have noticed is that, in all four of these types of exercise, remaining in touch with the sense of your body is very important. As discussed at the beginning of Chapter 2, this is the core of these practices. We are expanding the degree to which we can feel our body and this is intrinsically healing and grounding.

Before getting on to the Character Structures themselves, I want to mention Belly Breathing, as this is a core technique in many of the exercises. What I always find fascinating about teaching Belly Breathing is that pretty much everyone claims to already know it, yet in my experience pretty much no one actually does!

Belly Breathing

At least 99% of us get breathing wrong. That might seem like a pretty mad statement. I mean, it's an unconscious automatic process that we've been doing all our lives. So how could we possibly be getting it wrong?

There are many different muscles that we could use to expand and then deflate our lungs and thus take a breath. Our primate ancestors, when resting, used their abdominals, diaphragm and intercostals (the muscles between the ribs). So what do the majority of humans do? They suck air into their lungs by contracting and expanding the muscles around their throat, neck and shoulders – the scalenes, sternocleidomastoid, deltoid and pecs. This is the type of breathing that animals do when they need high levels of short-term energy. It's the type of breathing they do when their nervous system signals 'danger' and engages the fight or flight reflex.

The simple reality is that most humans these days are keeping themselves in a stress response throughout their day, solely through the way that they are using their bodies to breathe. We are breathing as though we were facing a threat. It has happened because our frontal lobes are constantly trying to control aspects of our personality and so they are not allowing us to breathe like healthy, relaxed animals. Over time, this simply becomes habitual, and we do it unconsciously.

To make the Bioenergetic and Reichian exercises in this book work well, you will need to learn and practise breathing with your belly - your abdominals. It's fine to also engage the diaphragm and the intercostals, but the belly muscles are what counts.

Stop reading for a moment and see if you can generate 5 breaths solely by moving your abdominal muscles. First, balloon your belly out, making it as big as possible. If your throat is relatively relaxed then your lungs will be drawn down and the vacuum thus created will fill with air coming silently in through your nose or mouth. Then, when full, relax and slightly compress your belly back again and, in like manner, the air will be pushed out again. Give this a try.

How was it? Could you breathe solely by utilising your belly muscles? It's a great idea to practise this a couple of times a day, just for a few minutes. Perhaps, after working on a laptop for a while, you take a 5 minute break, close your eyes and try to breathe in this way.

This, ideally, is how we will be breathing when we do the static Bioenergetics exercises in this book. With one difference. When resting, we generally breathe through the nose. We have our mouths slightly closed. This is fine but when doing the exercises in this book, we actually want to bring more energy into the core of the body. So, we do the exercises with the mouth slightly open. When our belly expands, it will draw air in through the mouth if it is open, and through the nose if the mouth is closed. So have your mouth slightly open when doing the static Bioenergetics exercises, unless otherwise stated.

Okay, now it's time to get to our first Character Structure – the Leaving Type.

The Leaving Type

**The
Leaving
Type**

Other names

Originally labelled by Reich as 'The Schizoid.' Other names that have been used over the years for this Character Structure include 'The Unwanted Child' or 'The Dreamer.'

Safety Strategy

What is fundamentally characteristic of this Type is that, when triggered, consciously or otherwise, their attention moves into their head and the world of thoughts, beliefs and judgements. They dissociate from the body.

Inner World

The inner world of this Character Type is marked by a feeling of unsafety, of fear. However, it is very common for this Character Type to not be consciously aware of the level of fear inside. Their experience is more likely to be that, despite all the exciting ideas and plans that they have, somehow none of them really happen. Something always seems to stop them from manifesting their ideas.

Description & Origins

It is generally believed that this pattern may have its origins as early as in the womb environment. The developing nervous system registers a sense of unsafety and begins to withdraw attention from the body. It may also begin in early infancy if there is simply a sense of emotional distance from the mother. In this latter case, it is similar to the Oral Character Structure. But, rather than fixating on 'connection,' the Leaving Type cuts off more completely from the world of feelings and simply inhabits the thinking mind.

Positive Qualities

People strong in the Leaving Type are great abstract thinkers and can be incredibly creative at a mental level. They may also have spiritual gifts and find themselves in possession of deep insights or the capacity to heal others.

Negative Attributes

People strong in this Type are dominated by fear, almost as though they actually have a layer of fear surrounding them. Others may notice this but they themselves are usually unaware of it.

This fear stops them from manifesting the ideas that they have, which are often really great ideas. They may be unaware that they are afraid of the world. Rather, it seems to them as though somehow something is always blocking them from the outside. Over time, this can lead to an underlying sense of frustration, resignation or depression.

People of the Leaving Type may also be aware of a lack of sensation in the body. Some of this Type may also find that it is hard to focus on one thing for any length of time. Their attention seems to flit around the place like a butterfly. This happens because if we focus on something, whilst feeling our body, feelings begin to rise. However, those of the Leaving Type may find it easy to focus on something as long as they're not feeling their body. But this can compound their fundamental state of dissociation.

People of this Type also often struggle with social contact. They prefer to spend time on their own or relating through social media or electronic devices where they feel safer and more in control.

They are also quite likely to be subject to nightmares, panic attacks and sudden bursts of strong emotion.

Three Channels

Here we look at how the typical Leaving Character rates in the 'Three Channels' system mentioned earlier on.

Grounding Channel – blocked

Belly-Throat Channel – blocked

Heart-Mind Channel – blocked or somewhat open

Typical Characteristics of Appearance

Here is a list of physical characteristics that someone strongly of the Leaving Type will likely have. Note that it would not be common for all to be present, rather a significant number.

- A frozen or shocked look in the eyes

- Shoulders habitually raised, as though in shock

- A body that looks disjointed, or perhaps not symmetrical

- Arms and legs often appear thin

- An emaciated, malnourished-looking body

- Skin colour may be excessively pale

- Hands and feet may be cold

- Chest and throat may appear constricted

- Feet clawing into the earth

- Body movements look mechanical

- Despite their skinny appearance, they may nevertheless be quite strong and athletic

Typical Characteristics of Behaviour

Here is a list of different behavioural characteristics generally associated with the Leaving Type. These are not specific to only this type and, as above, it is not likely that one person would have all of them.

- High levels of intuition, rather than gut feelings

- Acute difficulties in manifesting their ideas

- Difficulty dressing appropriately for different situations

- A fascination with abstract worlds – perhaps relating to spirituality, computer games or science

- May experience panic attacks or nightmares

- May experience bursts of rage which are quickly shut off

- May have a history of self-mutilating behaviour

- May be arrogant and dismissive of others

Typical Psychological Characteristics

This list relates to the inner world and experience of the Leaving Type. Like the other lists, it's unlikely that one person would ever manifest all these traits but the list is useful to provide a deeper understanding of the Type.

- They may have had an early sense of not being wanted

- They may have had a sense that their environment was not safe for them

- They may have received inadequate eye contact from the mother

- They may have experienced their mother as not wanting them

- Their inner world is likely marked by fear and anxiety

- They dissociate from the feeling of the body easily

- They may be hyper-vigilant

- They may get more pleasure from mental fantasies than from physical experience

- They may experience suicidal thoughts

- They may experience bursts of sudden emotion such as rage

- They may find themselves easily entangled in abusive relationships

Therapeutic Notes

In this section, I will give information about how to approach overcoming the part of us that tends to dissociate from the body.

The first thing to understand is that this behaviour is triggered by a sense of not being safe. It's a defensive strategy that is usually activated unconsciously. That's to say, we will likely not immediately be aware that we are being triggered. Our brain monitors our environment constantly, even when we sleep, and when it registers a sense of unsafety, it triggers the defensive strategy. We dissociate from the feeling of the body.

The path out of dissociation is easy to articulate – we need to re-inhabit our body and be able to stay there, even when triggered. This requires a certain vigilance. It also requires that we develop the means to determine when we are dissociated and when we are more present in the body. So the first thing is to make simply feeling the body a regular part of our daily life. We must come to appreciate our sense of the body. We have to come to the point where we derive actual pleasure from simply feeling the body.

There are no 'quick fixes' for healing the Leaving Type. It's important to proceed gently and with awareness. Indeed, if we push too hard, all we will achieve is simply more dissociation. I'm familiar with a lot of highly evocative therapeutic techniques, many from the world of breathwork and emotional expression. These techniques are usually not useful to treat the Leaving Type, for as soon as the technique begins their subconscious defences simply trigger them to leave the body.

Some breathwork practices, usually those with shamanic roots, actually use altered breathing to trigger a dissociated state with the intention that we develop spiritual insights. There is nothing wrong with these practices, but they are obviously not useful for treating the Leaving Type.

So, what techniques will be useful?

For a start, any technique which requires us to simply feel the body more deeply will be helpful. Having to direct our attention into parts of the body, and endeavour to keep it there, is great. An example of such a technique would be the popular 'body scan' technique often used by Buddhists. If you look online, you will be able to find many audio recordings of different body scans you can try out.

What happens in the Leaving Pattern is that our awareness goes up into our heads. There's nothing wrong with having awareness in the head. We do need to think. But if we can't easily bring it back into our body when we need to, then this is when it becomes a problem. When our throat has become 'blocked' – when we are just not comfortable expressing our feelings or speaking our truth – then this will prevent awareness from easily returning to the body. It makes sense. Between our head and the rest of our body is the throat area.

So, exercises that 'unblock' the throat can be especially helpful for the Leaving Type, provided that they don't bring up so much feeling or energy that they trigger dissociation.

Massage is truly great for people of the Leaving Type. Sensitive, intelligent physical contact reassures the nervous system that the body is a safe place to be. Regular massage, Deep Tissue Massage, Rolfing and myriad related techniques can work wonders for this Type.

Practising self-love is also important for the Leaving Type. Despite the gifts they may possess for intellectual pursuits or spirituality, this type invariably lacks self-love. They tend to try and make up for a lack of needed safe touch in early childhood by learning and learning, developing an immense intellect. But, finally, all they really crave is contact and a sense of loving themselves. If you're working on the Leaving side of yourself, then it's important to set aside some time daily to simply appreciate and be good to yourself. Even if your self-esteem is low, if you adopt behaviours associated with higher self-esteem – better clothing, better healthcare, treating yourself with care – it will improve. Like this, you can create your own inner shift.

Leaving Types, like most of the other Character Structures, also need grounding. The channel between the belly and the soles of the feet will be strongly blocked. Grounding exercises, such as walking on the earth with bare feet are great for this Type.

Playfulness is also important for the Leaving Type. They usually lacked good, simple friendships and connection in early life. Spending time being playful, especially with others, can work wonders.

Finally, anything which can support the Leaving Type to feel really a part of the physical world will be helpful. Good friendships and love relationships; a job where there is a connection to others and a sense of doing something valuable for society all will help greatly.

Exercises

We now come to the exercises. These are sequences of Reichian and Bioenergetic postures that, over time, will progressively release and integrate the negative aspects of a specific Character Structure.

Remember, do not just jump from one to another. Pick one and complete it many times on separate days before moving on to another. Exercises are listed alphabetically and there's no requirement to do them in any specific order.

- Belly Breathing, lying down
- Bow & Arch
- Devavani Child Gibberish
- Eye Rotation Exercise
- Forehead Ring Armour Release
- Gibberish
- Grounding through the Legs Sequence
- Kick-Out Grounding
- Ocular Ring Armour Release
- Oral Ring Armour Release
- Shoulder Opening Sequence
- Shoulders Raise
- Somatic Centre Sensing

The Oral Type

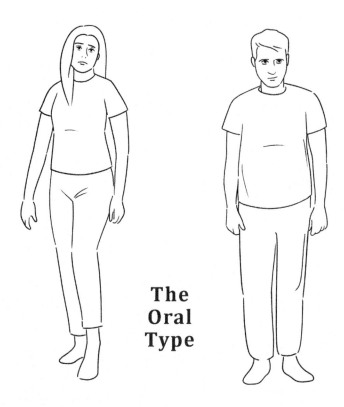

**The
Oral
Type**

Other Names

The Merging Pattern.

Safety Strategy

The fundamental safety strategy for the Oral Type is to look to others to source their own needs. The Oral type is fixated on connection and believes that, in order to survive, their connection to others is of absolutely vital importance. Whilst, as humans, we are of course social creatures and do need connection, the level of importance given to connection by Oral Characters is nevertheless exceptionally high.

Because of this extreme focus on the need to feel connected to others, Oral Types are frequently 'pleasers.' They often don't even consider who they themselves are as individuals. They are willing to simply be whoever they perceive the other as needing them to be, in order to maintain the connection.

Inner World

The inner world of the Oral Type is marked by a sense of lack, of never getting enough. Deep inside, someone strongly in this Type will believe, that no matter what happens to them, their needs will never truly get met.

Description & Origins

The Oral Character experienced an inadequate bond with the mother in the first year of life. Our DNA configures us to expect that our physical and emotional connection with our mother will be strong for our first year outside the womb. When this expectation is not met, a sense of 'lack' is stored in the body and the psyche.

Oral Subtypes

The defining trait of the Oral Character is their overwhelming need for connection with others. However, in human social culture, neediness is frequently seen as an impediment to creating connection. We are more likely not to be attracted to someone who we perceive as 'needy.' Thus, some Oral Characters have learned to mask this inner neediness, such that it does not hijack their ability to create the connections they need. These Types are usually termed 'Compensating Oral' Characters.

It's important to understand that, although there is a certain duplicity in this behaviour, there is rarely any conscious intent to deceive. The person simply adopts certain behaviours, usually during late adolescence, unaware of their deeper motivations.

The classic 'Compensating Oral' Type immerses themselves in taking care of others. By always 'being there' for people – whether as a professional carer or in friendships – they ensure that they are always 'needed.' By feeling constantly needed by others, they get the connection they themselves need, unaware that it is actually their own need that is motivating their behaviour.

In addition to the 'classic' type of Compensating Oral Character described above, there are also other personality types that have strong Oral traits that are covered over with avoidant or compensating behaviours. Most notably among these are 'narcissistic' personalities.

Many narcissists are strongly Oral. But they have learned to mask their inner neediness by exerting forms of subtle control over those they wish to keep close to them. They learn techniques to keep those they need in a state of dependency upon them – frequently making use of any pre-existing sense of low self-esteem in the other. In addition, narcissists will often become addicted to receiving attention from others, constantly trying to fill up the sense of a hole they have deep within.

It's important to realise that most narcissists actually do not do these behaviours consciously. They have little or no awareness of the level of personal neediness they have inside. They merely perceive the world and other people in a certain way.

When treating any type of Compensating Oral Character, it will inevitably be necessary for the compensating strategy that they are utilising to first be dismantled. This allows the underlying Oral trait to come to the surface, be experienced and, hopefully, accepted.

Positive Qualities

Oral characters have many qualities. Despite the fact that their personality is driven unconsciously, they can still contribute a great deal to relationships in particular. Typically, they make caring and responsive friends and lovers. They tend to be heart-centred and keen to know where others are at. They love intimacy.

In a society where many feel that deeper connections between people are not adequately fostered, Oral Characters are much valued for their willingness to seek out connection and intimacy wherever they can.

On the surface, the typical Oral Character is fixated with connection. But, deeper down, this fascination may run to greater extremes – into actual 'merging.' The fantasies of Oral Characters often contain strong themes of either merging with others, losing all sense of personal selfhood, or in some way dissolving. Thus, Oral Characters often find themselves attracted to spiritual belief systems, especially those which focus on the dissolution of personal selfhood – Buddhism, Non-dualism and similar. In spiritual environments, it will be normal to find a high percentage of Oral Types. The continued maintenance of spirituality in Western culture, with all the benefits that it brings, is in many ways due to the prevalence of Oral Characters in society.

Negative Attributes

Oral Characters have a deep, inner neediness created by the lack of expected connection with their mother in their first year of life. Their need for connection results in them negating their own real needs as individuals. They focus solely on adapting their own personality to 'fit in' with others. Thus, tendencies toward 'pleasing' are very strong within this Character Type. Similarly, emotions associated with confrontation – typically anger – are shunned.

Oral Characters find it almost impossible to stand up for themselves. Because so much of their personality is sourced in their need to get connection, the whole notion of confronting situations directly is often almost incomprehensible to them. They please. They are 'nice guys,' or 'good girls.' They tend to be compliant.

Oral Characters are also prone to depression, for reasons relating to the above traits. The human psyche may be considered a vessel, and one that needs adequate borders in order to function properly. Without a proper sense of boundaries, any energy which the vessel develops will quickly dissipate. This is just how it is with many Oral Characters. Being so reliant on staying open to connection, they cannot easily bring themselves to hold proper boundaries with the world around them. Thus, they struggle to hold their own energy. It seems to just leak away, leaving a periodic sense of low energy and a depressed attitude in its wake.

Three Channels

Let's look at how the typical Oral character is functioning in terms of these three channels.

Grounding Channel – blocked

Belly-Throat Channel – blocked

Heart-Mind Channel – open

Typical Characteristics of Appearance

Oral Characters have a general appearance that strongly suggests both submission and collapse. They rarely seem like people who could present any threat to anyone. Indeed, they appear to be seeking someone to cling to. Here is a brief list of classic physical characteristics of the Oral Type:

- A deflated, retracted chest

- A neck that reaches forwards, rather as an infant cranes for the nipple

- Weak-looking legs that seem barely capable of keeping them upright

- A somewhat protruding belly, sometimes the result of frequent snacking to try to 'fill the hole' inside

Typical Characteristics of Behaviour

Let's list some of the classic behavioural traits of Oral Characters:

- Their choice of clothing and general appearance may suggest an inability to look after themselves – a form of mother-seeking behaviour.

- Tendencies to become easily downcast and depressed, seemingly lacking the willpower to pick themselves up.

- Tendencies to please. Their first thought on meeting a new person may be "How can I become who this person needs me to be?"

- Tendencies to habitually seek something to fill an inner hole – food, drink, drugs, possessions, attention from others.

Typical Psychological Characteristics

Oral Characters have a deep, inner neediness created by the lack of expected connection with their mother in their first year. Here is a list of typical psychological characteristics:

- Habitual fantasising about merging with another or finding the perfect 'soulmate.'

- An inner world dominated by a sense of emptiness.

- Oral Types, deep inside, tend to believe that, no matter what happens, they are never going to get enough.

- Narcissistic traits of trying to fill an inner hole with attention from others are common.

- Tendencies towards addictive behaviours.

- A constant struggle to maintain healthy boundaries.

- Tendencies towards depression and listlessness.

Therapeutic Notes

There are two important directions that therapy for Oral Characters needs to take.

The first regards anger and boundaries. Orals invariably struggle to hold good boundaries and to adequately feel or express anger. They are driven by a need to try and remain open to connection, which can result in them getting hurt trying to resolve situations when actually they simply need to put up an adequate boundary. Exercises which allow Oral Characters to feel and express anger are very useful though. Similarly, exercises where they need to practise expressing boundaries will make it easier for them to do so in situations when they need to.

The second direction regards filling the sense of an inner hole that Oral Types invariably carry around, albeit largely unconsciously. These are exercises that take our minds back to early infancy and stimulate a sense of inner bliss. Sucking exercises are excellent. Likewise 'child gibberish' exercises. As the inner hole gets slowly filled up with blissful experiences, the sense of needing to please others to get needs met can dissipate.

Finally, once a sense of boundaries and more access to the bliss of infancy have been established, the final challenge for the Oral Type is to actually feel that hole inside. This has to happen gradually, less they simply develop Leaving traits or addictive behaviours. But being able to physically feel the sense of lack and stay present with that feeling until it passes will be a major milestone for the Oral Character.

Exercises

Let's list some excellent workouts for Oral Characters.

- Belly Activation Sequence
- Deep Neck Release Sequence
- Devavani Child Gibberish
- Dragon's Breath Exercise
- Kung Fu Punching with Sound
- Pelvic Floor Opening Sequence
- Rapid Inhale Belly breathing, lying down
- Right-to-Exist Exercise
- Sucking Gesture Exercise
- Teenager Release

The Endurer Type

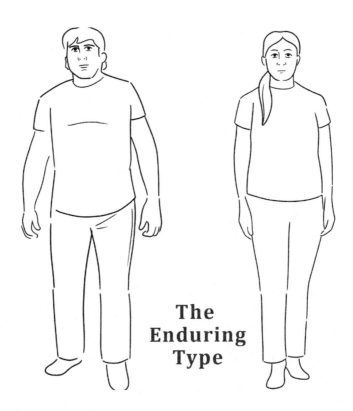

The
Enduring
Type

Other Names

This Character Type was originally labelled 'the Masochist' by Reich.

Safety Strategy

The fundamental safety strategies employed by the Endurer type are to avoid any form of confrontation, to bury their individuality deep inside of them and to seek to simply 'survive' life.

Inner World

The inner world of the Endurer Character is filled with angst and images of violence, strongly at odds with their outer appearance of being at peace. It is rather as though a battle is constantly going on within them between two opposing forces.

Description & Origins

Aged around 2-3 years, Endurers had their first attempts at self-expression so strongly negated by their parents that they learned that individuality was dangerous. They elected instinctively to bury their natural emotions, especially anger, deep within and to learn ways of simply surviving being alive.

This age period is the time when we first discover the word "No." It's commonly referred to by parents as the 'terrible twos,' for the way that children act out at this time. Aged one, if our mum wants to take us with her to the shops, we simply follow along. We have no sense that we might be able to resist or object. But, at around the age of two, we first get access to the concept of resistance and to the word, "No!" Now we can protest. We can rage about all manner of things in an entirely indiscriminate manner, simply experimenting and finding out what we can achieve with this new word and this new state of being.

This is obviously a testing time for parents. From having a largely passive baby to take care of, suddenly they find that they have this ball of rage on their hands, constantly acting out. They have to find a balance between curbing their child's volatility, by setting clear boundaries of acceptable behaviour, and still allowing the child to discover their own world and develop.

If the infant is allowed too much freedom at this age, he or she may grow up with no sense of necessary social boundaries and struggle to achieve maturity. On the other hand, if boundaries are too strongly asserted by the parents, the child may become overly fearful of expressing themselves at all.

It is this latter behaviour by parents, or other caregivers, which creates the Endurer Type. Having one or both parents who overly restricted their child's natural urge to resist, we will usually elect to surrender our individuality and simply comply with the authority figures. It's important to understand that this surrender is not through any form of psychological weakness. It is simply that, as small children, our parents' ongoing care is necessary for us to survive. If our brain registers the possibility that our parents will cast us out from their care, then most of us will simply comply. We elect to bury our natural anger deep within, associating it forever with extreme danger. We grow up believing that submission to the will of those over us is a prerequisite to survival.

Positive Qualities

Endurers make loyal companions, willing workers and caring friends. They are the guys (and they do tend to be male) who quietly get on with the job, whether it be on the shop floor, bringing up the family or being the friend that you can always rely on. They take on the drudge tasks and are always around. It would be hard to imagine Western civilization surviving for long without the input of the millions of Endurers who steadfastly continue working, come rain come shine. All they ask is to be treated with a modicum of respect and to be allowed to survive.

Unlike most of the other Character Types, Endurers are generally well-grounded individuals. Their safety strategy has been to push feelings down. Whilst this blocks the development of individuality, it does mean that energetically their centre of gravity is low down, near the ground.

Negative Attributes

Although Endurers indeed make loyal workers and friends, deep inside they harbour a multitude of resentments. They didn't become the way they are through self-awareness, rather through being – as they experienced it – brutalised into submission in early infancy.

The fear that they have of allowing their true feelings to show, especially anger, has been written deep into their musculature and now exists as a constant unconscious inhibiting mechanism. Unaware of their terror, they simply do what they need to do to survive, on autopilot. However, their inner world tends to still be filled with this suppressed conflict. They seek ways to release the cauldron of internal pressure without actually getting angry. Frequently this manifests as grumbling, complaining or subtle undermining behaviours.

At work, they will be the guys muttering in the background about the boss, or the system, as they go about their daily tasks. Any suggestion that they should actually do something about the complaints that they have might be listened to on the surface. But their intrinsic terror of confronting authority means that they will never act upon such suggestions.

Endurers who are married, or in a relationship, will often refer to their partner as "she (or he) who must be obeyed" or similar, trying to make light of their willing slavery.

Whilst terrified of confronting authority directly, Endurers will nevertheless frequently subtly undermine their boss, or the company, whenever the opportunity arises. They invariably do it in such a manner that it is not possible to pin such actions directly upon them.

In the above context, Endurers have a particularly difficult relationship with those of the Aggressive Character. The Aggressive will be determined to get his or her team functioning optimally, such that his or her plan can move forwards, full steam ahead. Whilst agreeing and compliant on the surface, the Endurer in the team will usually find a subtle way of holding things up, driving the Aggressive crazy, but doing it in such a way that he or she can never be seen by other team members as responsible. Aggressives and Endurers easily become locked into personal battles of will – the Aggressive determined to get the Endurer to move his or her ass and the Endurer determined to subtly evade having to do so.

Endurers thus also love to have rules and regulations that they can invoke (external protective authorities such as Health & Safety) to hold up the forward movement of a commercial concern.

The extreme level of angst that makes up the inner world of the Endurer may at times rise to levels that they find unbearable, leading to deep despair and suicidal thoughts. But Endurers are usually sufficiently grounded and caring to not follow through with such ideas.

Three Channels

Grounding Channel – open

Belly-Throat Channel – strongly blocked

Heart-Mind Channel – may be open or blocked

Typical Characteristics of Appearance

Whilst female Endurers certainly do exist, typically the Endurer is male. These are some typical physical characteristics:

- Heavy-set and musclebound. The Endurer acquires muscles not through working out but rather through suppressing the raging emotionality inside.

- Scary appearance. The heavy-set appearance of the Endurer will often make him appear scary.

- Short bull neck

Typical Characteristics of Behaviour

- Although they may look scary, Endurers are invariably passive in behaviour.

- They tend to complain and grumble

- They sometimes act as though they are stupid so that they don't need to take more responsibility

- At social gatherings, they are usually self-deprecating and will often portray themselves comically, as someone who obeys their spouse or boss because that's just how things are.

- Hardworking and reliable

- They exhibit little sense of joy in what they do or in life generally

- They may subtly undermine authority, recruiting others to their view.

Typical Psychological Characteristics

- The primary ambition of the Endurer is to simply survive life and to not be pushed or challenged. They will do whatever is necessary to achieve these aims.

- They submit to authority on the surface, with undermining behaviours existing underneath.

- There is huge anger deep inside, despite the surface of passivity. Yet, most Endurers, even when entering therapy, will be in absolute denial of this.

- Endurers have an especially dominating internalised voice of authority in their mind - the Freudian superego - constantly telling them which behaviours are okay and which are not.

- They have a deeply structured fear of confrontation and of getting angry.

- Whilst often behaving as though they would like things around them to change, Endurers will find fault or simply not comply with any actual strategy for change.

- Their inner world is marked by conflict and angst.

- They will frequently have 'revenge fantasies.' They love movies where the mild-mannered protagonist is finally pushed too far by the bad guys and enacts brutal revenge. Movies like 'John Wick' or 'Die Hard' are archetypal Endurer films.

Therapeutic Notes

The difficulty in treating Endurers lies in their deeply internalised rage – an anger that has sat there untouched since early infancy. Usually, they perceive themselves as people who simply 'aren't angry.' Their anger is so deep, so buried and so denied that it will inevitably be a journey to bring an Endurer towards its expression and integration.

Therapists who try too hard, too early to get an Endurer to express anger will simply be met with someone barely giving energy to the anger-producing exercise and who later shrugs their shoulders, as if to 'prove' that they simply don't have anger. It is thus important for therapists to not engage their Aggressive side when supporting an Endurer to change. Any pushing from the therapist will cause an Aggressive-Endurer relationship to develop (mentioned above) and this is unlikely to be fruitful.

A good way to start for the Endurer Type is to practice valuing their emotions. They learned in early infancy that their own feelings did not matter, that they had to simply comply to survive. Endurers need to take time to play and to feel, to recapture something of the magic of being a child, exploring and discovering their world.

If you are supporting an Endurer to change, you must repeatedly bring them back to appreciating their own feelings, and not simply negating them. Explain that what they think and feel has value and demonstrate this in how you interact with them. Over time, the Endurer will develop the confidence needed to go deeper into their own feelings and heal.

For this Character Type in particular, it is beneficial for them to learn about psychology in general and Character Structure specifically. Their true self has been buried so deep, it takes time and understanding for them to get interested in accessing their inner world.

As with the Leaving Type, slow progress over time is usually the best for the Endurer. Remember, they are usually well-grounded, function-ing members of society. They deserve respect as they slowly begin their own journey of self-discovery.

Therapists working with the Endurer Type need to keep in mind that a primary psychological issue for this type is a fear of authority figures. As infants, this Type elected to submit to authority as a way of feeling safe in the face of an overwhelming situation. The therapist will most definitely be regarded as another 'authority' in the mind of the Endurer. It is thus incumbent on the therapist to be clear, reasonable, uncharged and relatively unchanging in their general attitude when supporting the Endurer client to change. Explain clearly in advance any exercises be-ing proposed and allow the client complete freedom to take part or not. A big part of the healing is the therapist being so clear, supportive and honest that an Endurer client can have a positive experience of authority.

With regard to this latter point, it is also important to be aware that the Endurer's repressed issues with authority will inevitably be projected onto the therapist. It is common for Endurers to play subtle games with authority figures, as noted above. They may seek to cast the therapist into their own inner turmoil in cunning, manipulative ways.

Clients strongly in the Endurer type are often very challenging for therapists to work with. When therapists find themselves in despair or other deep, negative emotions when working with a specific client, it is frequently because an Endurer type has succeeded in sucking them into their own inner darkness, invariably a form of payback to authority in general. You do need experience and inner clarity to work with this Type.

Exercises

- Cervical 'Despair Release' Exercise
- Devavani Child Gibberish
- Dragon's Breath Exercise
- Free Writing Exercise
- Get Off My Back Legs Exercise
- Get Off My Back Shoulder Exercise
- Gibberish
- Mirror Affirmation Exercise
- Parent-Child Eye Exercise
- Pelvic Activation Sequence
- Push Breathing
- Right-to-Exist Exercise
- Trust Fall Exercise

The Rigid Type

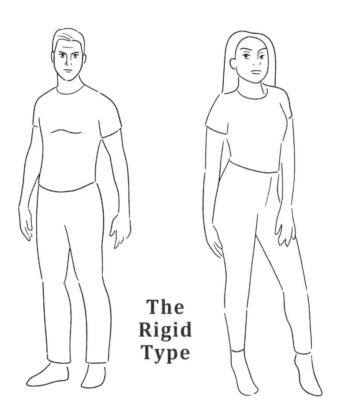

**The
Rigid
Type**

Other Names

I'm not aware of any other name that has been employed for this Character Type, though numerous Rigid subtypes have been discussed and identified over the years, whom we will discuss a little further on.

Safety Strategy

Someone strongly of the Rigid Type will have been taught early on that the spontaneity of feelings was not acceptable. They will have learned to survive by tensing their body and holding everything in, such that they could focus on achieving goals and performing well. Over time, this behaviour strongly suppressed their natural aliveness and gave them a rigid, robotic appearance that is mirrored in their personality.

Inner World

The Rigid Type is preoccupied with status and hierarchies. They daydream about moving 'up the ladder,' acquiring more wealth, more power or more attractive partners. Their inner world revolves around acquisition and ensuring that they avoid anything which could lower their social status.

Description & Origins

It is very important to recognise that, in moving on to considering the Rigid Type, we now enter the 'egoic phase' of child development. Individuals strong in the Leaving, Oral or Enduring types have highly diminished egoic strength. They will struggle to move in a coherent direction over time and to get their needs met. They lack drive. These early Types are 'pre-egoic.' The trauma takes place before their ego has begun to develop. That's to say, before they are 2-3 years old.

The Rigid Type is in a whole different category. Rigid Characters have ego. They have drive. The conditioning that they experienced happened after the initial stages of ego development were successfully completed.

As a child, the Rigid Type learned that, in order to get love, it was necessary to function well. Their parents rewarded them for behaviours deemed 'good' and punished them for behaviours seen as 'bad.' They learned the lesson. They got it. They understood that to succeed in life, their behaviour and how they were perceived by others were of paramount importance. Their feelings were rejected in favour of simple functioning. They went into the world believing that who they were did not matter. All that mattered was how they performed.

Rigid Types aspire to improve their social status. They play by the rules of society, as they perceive them, and they intend to win or to at least move up. They fixate on hierarchies and their perceived position within them, whether at work or in their love life.

The primary consideration for someone of the Rigid Type, when choosing friends or a partner, is whether the person will improve their social status. Likewise, at work, they do not seek a role that might give them contentment. They are simply concerned with moving up the promotional ladder.

Rigid Characters tend to model themselves on archetypal male and female figures. The men aspire to be 'very male,' the women to be 'very female.'

Rigid Characters are proud. They respect themselves for having risen to the challenges they've faced and disregard those whom they perceive as having failed to step up. This huge sense of pride in the Rigid Type allows standards to be maintained in society. Rigid Types make use of the sense of 'respect' to keep hierarchies in place.

Rigid Types thus thrive on challenges. They regard them as crucial to development and see them as having made them the man or woman they now are. They also regard it as important to challenge others, in order to see if the other can 'step up' and 'make the grade.' Those who succeed, the Rigid Type will be happy to accept as equals in the hierarchy. They will give diminished respect to those who fail, until such time as they can prove themselves.

Positive Qualities

Rigid Characters are the backbone of human society. They maintain standards and test those who wish to move up social hierarchies, to ensure they are ready and will fulfil their role well. They know and accept the rules of the game and they both play by them and uphold them. It is inconceivable that our society would have achieved its current level of development without large numbers of Rigid Types. They maintain standards. They constantly demand better results. They seek unrelentingly to improve their lifestyle and level of material assets. By demanding more, in a coherent and consistent manner, they pull the whole of the material world up around them.

Endurers do all the drudge work. Leaving Types are great at maths and science. Orals are excellent at art and creativity. But it is the Rigids that keep all this activity on track. They set standards and make sure everyone toes the line, keeping our culture moving forwards and upwards.

Negative Attributes

Rigid Types are obsessively materialistic. To them, the only thing that matters is how big something is, how many of them there are or how much it costs. Material values are the way that Rigid Types keep track of how well they are doing in the great competition for social status that runs constantly in their minds.

Rigid Types are strongly sceptical of anything which isn't purely rational. They have armoured over their own emotionality to such a degree that many would either deny the existence of feelings altogether or simply dismiss them as something that 'weak people' fall prey to. Rigid Types do not consider that human emotions are of much value. Feelings simply get in the way of good functioning and are to be avoided.

Rigid Characters find it very difficult to ask for help. To do so represents to them a drop in status, so they will invariably work very hard to try and resolve issues themselves without having to reach out. They are terrified of showing vulnerability. Faced with a choice between allowing themselves to be vulnerable and dying, many Rigid Types would choose the latter. To them, a drop in social status is anyway akin to death.

Rigid Subtypes

Rigid Characters were extensively studied in the mid to late twentieth century by an assortment of psychologists interested in this field. This resulted in various subtypes being identified and named.

In addition, as the formation of this Character Type takes place after the beginning of ego development, and because gender strongly influences this phase, Rigid male Types bear distinct differences from female Rigid Types.

This has resulted in 5 different types of Rigid Characters being regarded as existing. They are named thus:

- Phallic Narcissist (male)
- Hysterical (female)
- Masculine Aggressive (female)
- Passive Feminine (male)
- Obsessive-Compulsive (either gender)

Note here that the Masculine Aggressive Type is female, whilst the Passive Feminine Type is male.

I am not going to delve deeply into these subtypes, because I find this level of subcategorisation a little excessive and not really necessary.

Three Channels

Grounding Channel – closed or somewhat open

Belly-Throat Channel – somewhat open

Heart-Mind Channel – strongly closed

Typical Characteristics of Appearance

Because the development of the Rigid Character takes place after the beginning of our sexual development, male and female Rigid Types do not necessarily have the same physical characteristics. In the list below, I've identified those characteristics that are gender specific. Those not marked in this way apply to both sexes.

- A firmly set jaw, to keep moving forwards on their chosen track, in anticipation of resistance from others.

- Male Rigid Types tend to look very 'male,' female Rigid types very 'female.' Daniel Craig's "James Bond" and Victoria Beckham are excellent examples.

- High upper-body rigidity, especially in men.

- A hardened, mask-like face, which is usually attractive, but nevertheless clearly not used to showing much emotion.

- Women in this category have a high level of fluidity in their hip movements to demonstrate and make use of their femininity.

Typical Characteristics of Behaviour

Let's list some of the behaviour traits of Rigid personality Types.

- A willingness to stand up for what they believe to be right, seeking support for their positions from other Rigids where necessary.

- They demand more from others as a means to test the other's ability to 'step up.'

- When confronted, they set their jaw and stand firm. (Contrast this with the behaviour of Aggressive types under pressure.)

- Rigids have an obsessive need to demonstrate their essential masculinity or femininity to both themselves and others. The idea of not being gender-specific is both scary and incomprehensible to them.

- Rigid types tend to develop rituals and routines, partially as a means to keep their underlying repressed emotionality from interfering with their functioning. Along with things like always having a coffee at a certain time, these may also include compulsive behaviours like gambling, regular drinking, recreational drug use, the compulsive acquisition of material goods, or compulsive exercising.

Typical Psychological Characteristics

- They take pleasure in anything which affirms their intrinsic masculinity or femininity.

- Rigid males will seek casual sexual encounters until they find a female that they feel to be worthy of them, likely to produce good offspring, and to raise or at least maintain their social status. Such a woman will invariably be of the Rigid type also.

- Rigid females will test unrelentingly those males who pursue them, granting sexual favours only to those whom they feel to be worthy.

- They regard any situation that might make them feel vulnerable as threatening.

- They have a very low tolerance for uncertainty and will demand to know what's going on.

- They need a role in order to engage with life. The idea of living without a role would feel entirely meaningless to them.

- They have a strong distrust of emotionality and of people who they perceive as highly emotional.

- They worship rationality.

- Rigid types either deny the existence of their inner world of feelings, or simply regard it as something to be 'dealt with' such that it doesn't interfere with their good functioning. This causes excess emotional energy to develop, and they thus find ways to dissipate this. Typically, physical exercise and sports are popular to this end.

- Rigid Characters invariably regard therapy as something for 'weak people.' They would usually only consider seeing a therapist if they perceived themselves as in crisis.

Therapeutic Notes

As mentioned above, it will be rare for people strongly in this category to seek therapeutic help. To do so would be regarded as a sign of weakness and they far prefer to find ways to resolve their problems without needing to reach out and risk showing vulnerability. Indeed, typically, therapists' waiting rooms and group rooms are filled with people strongly in one of the pre-egoic Character Types – Leaving, Oral or Enduring.

However, the Rigid Type is also extremely practical and if he or she sees that they have a need for help that they can't get met otherwise, they will seek therapeutic assistance.

Because of the way that Rigid Types tend towards developing routines and behaviours which may border on being addictive, over time they do become more vulnerable to personal crises, perhaps related to drug use, gambling, drink-driving or over-spending. In addition, a sexual partner leaving or an expected promotion at work not happening may trigger deep feelings of unworthiness or low self-esteem that are more than they can cope with.

When they do reach out for help, it will usually be to someone that they perceive as an equal. This is in strict contrast to the Aggressive Type. Rigid males needing help will seek out a therapist of the same gender that they perceive as strong and professional. Rigid females will do the same.

In therapy, Rigid Types will invariably announce that they are merely seeking some means to quickly regain their normal functioning. They will not want to get too involved in their inner world and seek only a strategy to get them 'back on their feet.'

Therapists who like to lead clients into investigating their emotional depths, as many naturally do, may therefore quickly find themselves in a battle with the Rigid Type. They push the client to speak about their feelings. The client gives brief pat answers, interspersed with bursts of hostility. It's good to recognise that Rigid Type clients will treat any perceived attempt to get them to show vulnerability as an invasion that needs to be fought off.

For this reason, psychoanalysis is often of limited use with Rigid Types. It is too reliant on the client being open to speaking about their inner world and their childhood experiences. Therapies that work directly with the body may have more success, not least because they more re-semble the physical activities that Rigid Types already respect. Bioen-ergetics, Reichian Therapy, Myofascial Release and massage therapies like Rolfing and innumerable others can work well for Rigid Types.

As with the Endurer Type, it can be especially useful for the Rigid Type to develop a basic understanding of psychology. This can help them understand why it is beneficial to access emotions and to allow vulnerability.

Rigid Types are invariably used to acting aggressively. A therapist who is experienced in leading clients into the full-blown expression of anger can make use of this. By getting the Rigid type to go beyond aggressive posturing, and fully into expressing rage, huge releases of inner tension can occur. A subsidiary benefit of this is that, once some anger has been released, the Rigid Type will feel more comfortable with allowing themselves to be vulnerable and to talk about their inner world or childhood.

Rigid Types typically are very tense around the head, neck, throat and shoulders, the result of their mind being locked in a constant battle with all the emotions stored in their body. Regular massaging of trigger points in the scalp and in muscles like the Scalenes and the Sterno-cleidomastoid can help them greatly.

Reichian exercises that work with the armour rings around the fore-head, eyes, mouth and throat are all great. These exercises are usually a combination of specific breathing techniques done at the same time as tensing certain muscle groups in these areas of the body.

Bioenergetic exercises like the Dragon's Breath and the Right-to-Exist exercise also begin to invoke more expression.

When working with the Rigid Type it is useful to remember that they do have basic ego functionality. It is simply that they have no experience of deeper emotions and so, naturally, a layer of fear has accumulated. Once they can open up certain muscle groups, gain experience of feeling more emotion, and see that they can show more emotion without the world opening up and swallowing them, they will be fine.

Exercises

- Bow & Arch
- Cervical 'Despair Release' Exercise
- Chest Ring Armour Release
- Croak Breathing
- Cry Breathing
- Devavani Child Gibberish
- Dragon's Breath
- Forehead Ring Armour Release
- Get Off My Back Shoulder Release
- Get Off My Back Leg Release
- Gibberish
- Kick-Out Exercise
- Kundalini Shaking
- Laughing Exercise
- Ocular Ring Armour Release
- Oral Ring Armour Release
- Pelvic Activation Sequence
- Push Breathing
- Shoulder Opening Sequence

The Aggressive Type

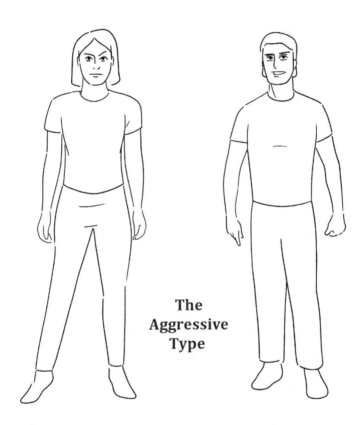

**The
Aggressive
Type**

Other Names

Formerly known as the 'Psychopath,' and later referred to as the *Leader*, *Dominator* or *Inspirer*, the origins of this Type are not clear to me. It is not present in Reich's original work, *Character Analysis*. Nor does it appear in Lowen's *The Language of the Body*. But, whatever its origins, it has certainly stuck and is included in all modern thinking on Character Structure.

Safety Strategy

The Aggressive Character has learned that the best way of dealing with any perceived sense of threat is to be proactive. Their fundamental safety strategy is to channel their energy up their body and to their face and chest, creating a powerful and charismatic front with which to face and dominate the world. They are both leaders and charmers, either overtly or subtly pulling you into their dominion before you even realise that it's happened! To do this effectively, Aggressive Types also need to think very quickly and plan out their response to ongoing situations.

Aggressive Types have a chameleon-like quality to them. They adjust the front they present to the world, depending on the situation they face. Where the Rigid Character simply tenses up and hardens to a challenging situation, the Aggressive will fluidly shift personality – at times commanding and authoritative, at times charming or seductive.

Inner World

The inner world of the Aggressive Type is marked by constant mental activity and change. Their brains are adapted to rely heavily on dopamine and adrenaline. They thrive on challenge and on pitting their wits against a world that they perceive as both antithetical and full of people inferior to them.

Description & Origins

As mentioned earlier, this Type is not found in Reich's original book, *Character Analysis*. Whilst, to my mind, the Aggressive is most definitely a distinct Character Type, and does relate to a fundamental Safety Strategy, it is also the case that it is not so straightforward to attribute its origins to a specific childhood situation.

Aggressive Types, like the Rigids before them, will also avoid therapy if they possibly can. One result of this is that we therapists don't have so much data about the typical Aggressive Character's childhood.

However, what is commonly noted with this Type is that there was a significant and rapid loss of trust in an authority figure, usually a parent, and usually between the ages of 5 and 12. Perhaps, as the child, the Aggressive completely doted on their mother. Then one day they became aware that they were simply being used as a pawn in some form of power struggle going on with the father. Or perhaps they were totally trusting of their father, until one day he turned on them irrationally when in a bad mood.

What is common is this sense of an early, deep love being suddenly torn asunder and leaving the child feeling bereft and with no one to console them. Internally, the child elects to never trust anyone again and to never allow themselves to feel so vulnerable. They resolve to become heavily self-reliant and determined to succeed at all costs. They gave their love to the world unconditionally and were rejected. Now it's time for payback. They will go it alone and they will show the world that they are not someone to be treated in this way.

Driven by a need to avoid the feeling of vulnerability, the Aggressive will seek power unrelentingly. The wound they carry inside took place well into the egoic phase of child development. So they have ego. They have drive. They are unlikely to stop until they have got themselves into a position of relative invulnerability – a place from where they feel that they call the shots – and where they feel safe.

As mentioned above, the Aggressive character is strongly motivated by challenge. Feeling themselves to be up against the wall, under pressure, on the edge of death, feeds their system with certain brain chemicals and gives them the sense that they are really alive.

Whilst challenge is, to my mind, indisputably a central aspect of personal development, the Aggressive Type frequently becomes addicted to taking risks. They have learned to channel repressed emotional energy up their body, as opposed to simply allowing the human feelings inside. This happens most easily when they're under fire, on the edge. If things get too humdrum, a sense of emotional pressure builds up inside of them, threatening to break their state of invulnerability. The result is a constant need to take risks, motivated unconsciously by a need to avoid feeling vulnerable.

This addictive state has been the downfall of many Aggressive Characters. Their need for risk-taking frequently leads them into criminal acts or drug use. Finding themselves in court, they may even refuse proper representation, preferring again to go it alone, partly through their difficulty to trust others and partly through their love of being on the edge. Needless to say, this rarely ends well.

Aggressives struggle deeply with normal human friendships. They far prefer to be in a role where others are attracted to them, but they can remain aloof and in control. The Aggressive Character prefers to have people following him or her, in a state of admiration, rather than to develop close friendships. They love to be influencers, politicians, entrepreneurs, rockstars – essentially anyone with status. Over time, this lack of people in whom they can confide – with whom they can share their struggles and fears – again tends to lead the Aggressive into difficult situations. Drug use is very common with Aggressive types, attractive for its ability to briefly bolster their need to feel invulnerable.

Psychopath – Really?

I want to mention one hugely complicating factor when discussing the Aggressive Character Structure – the original designation of 'psychopath.' This heavily pathologising term makes discussing and understanding the Aggressive Type difficult in two ways.

Firstly, unlike the names of the other Character Types – Leaving, Oral, Enduring and Rigid – the term 'Psychopath' is also a DSM psychiatric designation. DSM is the Diagnostic & Statistical Manual – the standard Western manual that designates and describes psychiatric conditions. The term 'psychopath' (sometimes 'sociopath') thus has a standard meaning in psychiatry as well as in Character Structure. These meanings are different but by no means unrelated. Anyone scoring high in the various psychological tests to attribute psychopathy – such as the Psychopathic Personality Inventory (Revised) – would very likely also score high in Aggressive personality traits. That, however, does not indicate, by any means, that they are necessarily a danger to society.

Secondly, the term 'psychopath' is so pathologising, especially in the wake of the numerous serial killer documentaries and movies, that the term has to my mind no therapeutic value. For whom would it be beneficial to receive the diagnosis 'psychopath?'

Positive Qualities

Aggressive Characters are dynamic leaders, entrepreneurs, powerful speakers and inspirational motivators. They move our energy, get us up on our feet, engaged with life. They take risks. They add colour. They never say die, never give up. They fight to the last. They are the quintessence of the "Captain Kirk" spirit – ever ready to boldly go where no man, or woman, has gone before.

All human culture needs its Endurers and its Rigids, to get stuff done and maintain standards. But what distinguishes modern Western culture from all other human cultures is the high proportion of Aggressive Types. Without them, and the culture of risk-taking that they embody, America would never have become the world superpower that it has.

Negative Attributes

Up on stage, in front of the crowd, the charisma and presence of an Aggressive Character can lead us into a deep recognition of the incredible experience of being human. But they themselves are left out of the show. Whilst we're all hugging and sharing in the aftermath of a dynamic concert or motivational speech, they are backstage, behind a wall of security, preferring their own company and choice of drugs.

This is the paradox of the Aggressive Character. They can achieve what we only dream of achieving. But, because of the way in which they are driven, it fails to give them the lasting satisfaction they seek.

Aggressive Characters cannot really access pleasure in the normal human sense. They learned to channel all their emotionality, as energy, up their body and to the front. They seek sex, not for pleasure but rather for a sense of power. They seek followers, instead of friends. They drive us forward, but they themselves feel empty inside.

The antipathy that Aggressive Characters feel towards those they perceive as 'mere mortals' can be considerable. Lacking empathy is actually not, in my opinion, an Aggressive trait, despite what some other commentators have written. But an Aggressive without empathy is potentially a dangerous proposition. Driven to extremes, without a means to feel how their actions affect others, they can wreck lives and leave complete chaos in their wake.

Aggressive Types can be manipulative and Machiavellian. Their minds work ultra-fast to determine their best strategy in any given situation.

On the surface, it might seem that the ideal role for the Aggressive Character would be as the CEO of a company, or at least high up in the boardroom. However, people high in this Character Structure are usually too unstable to gain, or hold down, such a role. Some level of the Aggressive Character is certainly useful to make one's way quickly up the corporate ladder. But too much will be debilitating.

Aggressive Types tend towards arrogance and to regarding others as inferiors.

When Aggressive Types make mistakes, it is often not easy for them to learn from them. They would need to admit that they were wrong and many prefer to 'double down' on their strategy, determined against all odds to prove that they were right all along!

Many Aggressive Types rarely experience self-doubt.

The regular need for thrills and challenges will eventually bring many who are high in Aggressive traits into trouble. They may break the law habitually. Once they pass through a previously held behavioural boundary, such as drug use or crime, they are likely to go further. It's only a matter of time before their acts begin to catch up with them.

Three Channels

Grounding Channel – Usually closed but perhaps slightly open

Belly-Throat Channel – Open

Heart-Mind Channel – May be closed or somewhat open

Typical Characteristics of Appearance

- A striking front aspect is common amongst Aggressive Types. They direct their energy to the front top half of their body, to the chest and face.

- Less grounded Aggressive Types tend to have an almost triangular upper body shape, with a narrow waist and underdeveloped legs.

- Some Aggressives however prefer seductive fluidity rather than appearing powerful and prestigious. The body shape of this type will appear less focused on the top half and more flexible in the hips.

Typical Characteristics of Behaviour

- Fast-thinking and chameleon-like, Aggressives love to jump into new situations to see if they can hold their own or dominate the scene.

- In a new social environment, they may find ways to marginalise anyone they perceive as competing with them for control or attention.

- They seek admirers and followers. To achieve this end, they may appear open and friendly and give individuals a large amount of attention to begin with. Once hooked, the individual is invariably pushed towards the back of the Aggressives interests.

- Aggressives live life on the edge.

- Aggressives may pursue sex in a predatory fashion, though this will be more for the sense of power it gives them, rather than for pleasure.

Typical Psychological Characteristics

- Aggressives have a deep, psychological need for power over others. This serves two purposes. It helps them to feel safe and it also serves as a form of payback over the figures in their childhood who they believe slighted them.

- Aggressives are terrified of not moving forwards, psychologically or physically. They cannot bear to go without a dopamine fix for very long. They fear collapsing into a state of low self-esteem should they ever stop moving, externally or internally.

- Aggressive Types never allow themselves to feel 'cornered' – unable to escape or extricate themselves from a situation, should the need arise.

- Aggressives, in direct contrast to Rigids, will find it impossible to accept anyone as having authority over them. Rigids will accept authority from another as long as they respect them or the structure surrounding them.

- In like manner, Aggressives have literally no respect for rules, whether social or legal. Rules are for other, lower beings. They might appear to abide by them at times, but that is just for show. Similarly, they have no respect for those who follow rules. They regard the compliance of others as indicative of their inferiority.

- Whilst powerful, seductive and charismatic, Aggressive Types are by no means necessarily malignant. In my opinion, they actually only pose a potential problem to society when their Heart-Mind Channel is closed and they run into a situation that sends them over the edge.

Therapeutic Notes

Those strong in the Aggressive Character, predictably enough, will rarely seek therapy. Whilst Rigid Types will accept the need for support when they see no alternative, Aggressives will usually just go into denial when situations turn severely against them. If legally bound to attend psychological evaluation, Aggressives will simply play games with the psychiatrist.

However, there certainly are Aggressive Types who, having achieved the status and wealth they originally craved, turn their attention to the inner journey and seek out the challenge of becoming engaged in therapy. Becoming aware that they cannot allow themselves to feel vulnerable or controlled, for example, some Aggressives will see this as a challenge that they naturally wish to overcome. They seek to learn how to become vulnerable.

Seeking a therapist, the Aggressive Type, unlike the Rigid Type, will initially choose someone that they sense that they can control. Rigid Types will seek a therapist they perceive as an archetypal male or female type – someone they can respect. Aggressives will seek someone that they feel they can run rings around should they need to. The typical Aggressive fear of being cornered means that, in a therapeutic situation, they need to feel that they are in the driving seat.

Thus, should you be working with someone strongly of the Aggressive Type, you need to clearly indicate, even though they will not acknowledge it, that they are in control. Amplifying your own caring side, and reining in any aggressive side you might have, will also be of value, at least when getting started.

As with Rigid Types and Endurer Types, it can be really useful for Aggressive Types to understand their condition and what likely formed it. Developing understanding at a mental level is very useful. It reassures people when the going gets tough and helps them stay the course.

Core psychological tasks for the Aggressive Type include grounding, allowing vulnerability, learning to feel and express their emotions and allowing themselves to be still – physically and mentally.

Unlike the other four Character Types, the Aggressive does not suppress their energy, as does the Endurer. Neither do they dissociate from their feelings (Leaving), obsess about connection (Oral Type), or simply harden themselves (Rigid). The Aggressive Type is alone in that they allow the flow of emotional energy through the body but they channel it away from human emotionality.

Thus, for the Aggressive, simply learning to take time to investigate their emotions before acting is a very useful direction. As a therapist, this should be constantly encouraged. Before you suddenly rushed out the door, what were you actually feeling in that interaction with your staff member? Please take your time to unravel the situation a little. Before you launched into that tirade at the bar last week, that you've just described to me, was there anything that you think could have triggered you? Once the Aggressive Type becomes interested in their inner world, a big part of the therapy has been achieved.

For anyone concerned about the level of Aggressive Character in their own personality, as I have been at times, it can be very useful to understand that pretty much all the strongly negative traits associated with this Type can only manifest when they have a closed heart centre. When the Aggressive Type is shut off from his or her empathy and meets a situation that is very challenging for them, this is when the descent into dangerous behaviour can occur. The empathetic response keeps them human and allows the Aggressive Type to make use of their considerable gifts.

Thus, it is an excellent 'insurance policy' for the Aggressive Type to invest time to develop empathy and the capacity to open his or her heart.

Relating to this, developing the capacity to trust others is vital for the Aggressive Type. As noted earlier in this section, the Aggressive Type very often suffered a huge wound around trusting a parent, or other caregiver, early in life. They trusted someone totally and were let down. They resolved to go it alone and never trust another. But this is not a viable life strategy for the long-term. It is a really great choice for the Aggressive Character to work on this wound and to slowly but progressively develop the capacity to trust other humans. Gradual steps are the way forward here. Trust comes from deep inside the felt sense of the body and cannot be pushed. It takes time to feel safe.

Working on grounding is also vital for the Aggressive and will support them to both allow more vulnerability and to feel okay to explore their underlying emotionality. Grounding is vital for anyone to go deeper into feelings, as it provides a sense of safety. When grounded, we feel internally that the emotion underneath, whatever it may be, will not overwhelm us and drag us down. As a therapist, we want to get the belly centre and the whole grounding channel – from the belly to the soles of the feet – open. I will list some great Bioenergetic exercises for this in the Workouts section below.

The Aggressive Type is so used to directing their energy to the front of their body that it's common for them to not feel much of anything in the area of their back. Exercises which open up the muscles of the back and allow feeling to return are really useful and will help them to feel more okay with simply trusting life.

Finally, allowing more stillness in their life can be transformational for the Aggressive Character. People high in this Character invariably struggle to simply be with themselves. They constantly need to 'do something' – either physically or mentally. Simple sitting, or mindfulness practices, can be an excellent challenge for them. I initially suggest that they try these for just 5 minutes and then work up. It's important to understand that sitting there making a thousand plans for the future is not meditation!

As an actual meditation practise, I recommend sitting, belly breathing and feeling the movements of the abdomen. I also recommend moving slowly around their space, taking in everything that is happening, a simple mindfulness practice.

Exercises

As mentioned above, core therapeutic directions for the Aggressive Type are trust, grounding, stillness and empathy. Let's take a look at some great workouts to work towards these ends.

- Belly Breathing Sitting Meditation

- Cry Breathing

- Crying Exercise

- Grounding through Legs sequence

- 'I feel…' Mirror Exercise

- 'I Need To Love' Mirror Exercise

- Kick-Out Exercise

- Kneeling Trust Fall Exercise

- Somatic Centre Sensing

- Spinal Feeling Journey Exercise

- Sucking Gesture Exercise

- Trust Fall Exercise

Compound Types

Now that we have worked through the 5 basic Character Structures, taking the time to unravel each from the different perspectives of infant experience, behaviour, psychology and appearance, we can take a look at 'Compound Types.' By this I mean considering persons who manifest a high amount of two different structures. Taking the time to do this can be useful for several reasons.

Firstly, because nowadays there most definitely are people simultaneously high in two or more Structures. I explore how changes in society have resulted in changes in our Character Structure in a piece in Chapter 11.

Secondly, and in a sense more importantly, because understanding how different Structures might integrate within one individual can lead to a deeper understanding of Character Structure itself.

Finally, there are limits to how much you can learn about Character Structure from simply reading about it. That is where most of us start from. But at some point we need to make this system more real and vital, and seeing how Compound Structures manifest is an excellent and engaging way to do this.

What I also find fascinating about Compound Structures is the way that some of them manifest this 'one foot on the gas pedal, one on the brake' aspect. There is drive within the individual but they struggle to go anywhere in life. These are invariably Compound Structures that are a mix of egoic and pre-egoic Types.

When working with Compound Structures, it is the rule that, ideally, you work with the earliest pattern first. That's to say, in an Oral-Rigid personality, you work first with the Oral component; in a Leaving-Oral, you work first with the Leaving aspect.

Be aware also, that clearing one Character Structure will frequently lead to another, later one taking its place! Someone high in the Leaving Pattern, for example, as they begin to come back into the body, may become quite Rigid or Aggressive!

Okay. All that said, let's jump into Compound Characters. To avoid repetition, the notes here will be less extensive than those for the individual Types. I will restrict information to three categories – Manifestation, Understanding and Treatment Notes.

Leaving Compound Structures

There are four possible Compound Structures that utilise the Leaving Pattern. These are Leaving-Oral, Leaving-Enduring, Leaving-Rigid and Leaving-Aggressive. Of these, the first and the third are fairly common and the others less so. But as mentioned above, we will look at all because doing so will support us to develop a better overall understanding of Character Structure.

What is common to all these Structures is that they have this 'Leaving' component – the tendency to utilise dissociation from the body as the primary safety strategy.

Let's go through them.

Leaving – Oral

Manifestation

This classic pattern is famous for manifesting in a certain way. The individual finds themselves in a fundamentally depressed state that is occasionally broken by bursts of intense and inspiring mental activity. Whilst in one of these states, they will frequently develop an exciting vision of something that they could manifest in their life. This vision is so inspiring that it completely galvanises them out of their depression and for a period of time they are filled with energy.

However, at the first sign of trouble – something not going the way they planned – they find the energy drains completely out of them. They collapse energetically, losing both the will and the ability to continue moving forwards. They find themselves back in their fundamentally depressed state, surrounded by whatever is left of their plans. At some point, another vision will begin to manifest and the process repeats.

Understanding

Examining this Compound Structure, it is relatively easy to see how the two elements play out. The Oral component simply sits in the relatively depressed state. (Note that this does not mean that they are necessarily clinically depressed. Rather than they feel listless, down and unengaged with life, lacking the drive to move forwards.) The Leaving component provides the occasional bursts of exciting vision.

It may be that they hear about a new project or a new therapy, make a new friend, or just come up with a really exciting idea. It may be simply some cyclical function of their brain chemistry. But the vision will always be mental – ideas based. They get inspired. But they cannot maintain that inspiration, and the energy that comes with it, in the face of even the slightest setback.

Their imagination will be keeping them engaged and moving forwards, always looking into the future and seeing themselves as successful, with a new partner, new freedom, whatever. As soon as this imagined vision of how things will be meets an actual situation that does not correspond to it, the energy drains right out of them.

Treatment Notes

The Leaving-Oral Character is overly reliant on imagination to pull them out of their underlying depressed state. Our mental facility to imagine is just not strong enough a workhorse to function for very long in the reality of the modern world. Any vision we wish to manifest will meet regular bursts of 'pushback.' This is just how it is. If we do not have the resilience and the wisdom to know what we need, we will inevitably collapse in the face of these constant knock-backs.

There are many entrepreneurial types who manifest this pattern quite strongly. They tend to shift between highly engaged, creative states to apathy and disengaged depression in regular cycles. When someone of this Type does become successful, it's usually because their ideas make enough money for them to surround themselves with a team of people who can keep the project moving forwards during the times when they feel drained of energy and vision.

The Leaving-Oral Type must develop more grounding. Moving forwards in life can never be achieved by imagination alone. We have to develop discipline and self-honesty. We need grounded awareness.

Remember the basic rules for treating the Leaving Character Type:

- The goal is to bring more awareness into the body, especially the lower half, from the belly down.

- Work gently. There's no point in intense sessions if you simply find yourself dissociating.

- Working at the throat can help attention and awareness, that has become 'stuck' in the head, return to the body.

- Practice belly breathing. Learning to breathe consciously, with the muscles of your abdomen, should be a core practice for those with the Leaving Structure.

Once the Leaving component is worked on in this way, and they feel much more present in the body, the Oral side can be worked on too.

Leaving – Enduring

Manifestation

From a fairly common pattern, Leaving – Oral, we move onto a Structure that I actually can't ever recall encountering. I discuss it briefly because, as mentioned, it will serve to further our understanding of Character Structure.

The reason why this pattern is so rare will likely be apparent to anyone who is becoming versed in Character Analysis. The Leaving Structure is all about taking attention up out of the body and into the head. The Enduring Structure, however, is all about pushing attention down towards the ground. Those with the former are ungrounded and fearful of life, whereas Endurers are very grounded but scared of their own individuality.

The reality is that it is not easy to adopt two such opposing Safety Strategies. Either we take the attention up, or we push it down. Of course, as a child, we may have experienced both a sense of unsafety as a very small infant, and having a parent who crushed our first resistance to their authority when aged 2. But, in such circumstances, I find it more likely that the person would simply remain as the Leaving Type, this being the first strategy adopted. In fact, the tendency to dissociate from the body would in my opinion likely be reinforced by any overbearing parental control being applied a little later on down the line.

Leaving – Rigid

Manifestation

Now we arrive at a much more likely combination – a personality that has learned to dissociate in very early infancy, but only partially. As their ego begins to develop, they learn to bolster up their sense of safety in the world by rigidifying their character – armouring up.

The classic Leaving-Rigid Type has an appearance that suggests someone operating in their own world – detached from those around them. A highly functioning unit that nevertheless appears insular and who will avoid deeper connection with others, both physical and emotional.

Understanding

This Character Type is one of the most common now being churned out by our 21st-century society, all over the globe. Working on a screen each weekday, and using the same technology to get social contact when not working, has created considerable dissociation from the body in this character.

Treatment Notes

The bottom line for this Character Type is self-challenge to get more physical connection and to allow more emotional vulnerability. Once their heart centre can begin to open, they will become amazed and fascinated by the inner world of deep connection that exists inside. They may have to consistently push things to the limit emotionally to find the places inside themselves where they can break through the rigidity to unrestrained feelings.

Leaving – Aggressive

Manifestation

The Leaving-Aggressive Pattern, like the Leaving-Enduring above, is not on the surface a likely combination. If all of one's energy has been taken up into abstract mental worlds, it can't very well be channelled into the chest and the face. Yet, like the Leaving-Rigid, there certainly are characters, strong in Leaving tendencies who nevertheless have an ego and have developed it aggressively.

Understanding

One might perhaps consider the social media 'keyboard warrior' to be an example of the Leaving-Aggressive Type. Happy to engage in a huge war of words online, yet terrified of the prospect of normal social contact. However, I see this type of character as simply dissociated and angry. They lack the charisma and charm of the genuine Aggressive Character.

Where I do see the Leaving-Aggressive Character is in people, originally strong in the Leaving Type, who are now transitioning out of that and whose underlying Aggressive traits are coming to the surface.

They find themselves more confident in social situations – no longer locked in the classic Leaving Pattern state of fear. They begin to experiment with becoming more powerful and more charismatic. It is a bizarre experience for them, being used to being so shy and then suddenly discovering that they can shape their experiences with others by adopting the Aggressive Character as a strategy.

This transition from a state of acute social nervousness to outgoing self-confidence can be so striking that it has led to a whole industry of self-help gurus selling techniques to quickly facilitate change.

Shy young men, in particular, learn strategies to forge social or sexual connections with women through simply adopting an aggressive, confident persona.

Treatment Notes

Whilst adopting an Aggressive Character Style can support people who lack the confidence to come out of themselves, this is not without issues. What tends to happen is that the shy, fearful person still exists inside underneath the front through which they've learned to interact with society.

Men may learn techniques to 'pick up' women but still cannot forge satisfactory love or sexual relationships because there is only so much that can be achieved through a front. At some point, we have to investigate our inner world more deeply. This cannot be avoided. Learning 'hacks' to appear confident or outgoing can at best only be a stop-gap measure. It's no substitute for an integrated personality that can both be open and hold boundaries.

The Leaving aspect of the psyche needs to feel the body more. There has to be a commitment to work with this. The throat needs to open, likewise the rings of lateral armouring around the forehead, eyes and mouth. Adopting an Aggressive persona is okay to improve social connections but the work must continue in the background.

Oral Compound Structures

We have already looked at the Leaving-Oral Structure, leaving us with three other Oral Compound Structures: Oral-Enduring, Oral-Rigid and Oral-Aggressive.

What is common to these Structures, of course, is that they all have this sense of 'deep lack' to them – the defining trait of the Oral Character. They all feature this inner neediness that may be on the surface or hidden beneath 'compensating' character traits, such as constantly giving to others or narcissism.

Let's take a look.

Oral – Enduring

Manifestation & Understanding

Someone high in both Oral and Enduring traits will likely be eking out their existence in a state of both pleasing and desperate neediness. They will probably be willing to do whatever it takes to create a connection with others, their own personality and personal needs submerged so deeply that they have literally no idea that they even exist at all. Avoiding confrontation and 'pleasing' will have become utterly ingrained in their personality. They are on a flat-out survival trip and are happy with any scraps that life tosses them.

The Oral-Endurer type is one stereotype among those who become addicted to opioids. This class of drugs both temporarily fills the inner sense of lack and suppresses emotions. It thus keeps both the Oral and Endurer sides from making chaos of the person's inner world. It is much more common in men.

Such a user is often the 'gentle giant' type, who seems both sleepy and sensitive, perhaps a beautiful being. But no matter what, he just can't seem to get clean from drugs or get his life together.

Treatment Notes

As is the case for all Compound Structures, ideally we seek to treat the earliest Structure first. As the Character Structures run Leaving, Oral, Enduring, Rigid, Aggressive, this means the Oral aspect to the person.

So, excellent exercises include those which work with expressing boundaries, increasing grounding through the legs, and filling up that inner hole where we didn't get our need for connection with the mother met as an infant.

Remember, when it comes to expressing and holding safe boundaries, to also include verbal exercises, rather than bodywork alone. Oral-Endurers need to learn and practice simple, clear ways to state needs. Verbal techniques like Nonviolent Communication (Marshall Rosenberg) can be excellent. When learning to hold safe boundaries, the focus should not be on strength but rather on clarity. You don't need to forcefully keep people from invading your physical or psychological space. Rather, you need to state clearly what you need, ideally with little charge in your voice.

For this Compound Structure, it will be quite a journey, and it will take time. The events of their childhood, and their natural disposition toward creating safety, have resulted in them burying themselves deep within, where no one could ever hurt them again. Regular work and practice, and ongoing positivity and support, will be needed.

Oral – Rigid

Manifestation

Now we come to a Compound Structure that is common in 21st-century society – the Oral-Rigid. This Structure results in a person with a deep sense of neediness inside that has been rigidified over.

The classic narcissist is Oral-Rigid. They have learned a specific strategy to deal with their Oral wounding, such that they can get the connection with others that they need, but without having to feel vulnerable. They have learned to control certain types of other people.

Understanding

The Oral component of this Structure is that gap where we did not get the connection with our mother in the first year of our life. This creates a sense of deep inner neediness, often manifesting as the underlying belief that, no matter what we get or achieve in life, it will just never be enough.

As the Oral-Rigid type reaches adolescence, he or she realises that acting out their needy side is not attractive. They see that it actually results in them losing the friendship or love connections they so deeply crave. Feeling the predicament that their Oral side has put them in, the Oral-Rigid elects to harden over their needy side, to bury it beneath bodily armouring. They become like a vulnerable child living inside a tank.

But, of course, they still need people, even though they may have little or no conscious sensation of this need. They learn strategies to bind others to them in manipulative or unhealthy ways. 'Gaslighting' is a classic example of this type of manipulation. By keeping a partner or friend in a state of low self-esteem, though regularly bringing them down in subtle ways, they create the sense in the other that staying in connection with the Oral-Rigid is the only way that they can survive. Of course, they need to find someone who is already vulnerable to collapse and low self-esteem.

In addition, the Oral-Rigid seeks to try and fill up the gap inside them by getting attention from others. We learn as children that if we can't get the love that will truly nourish us, then getting attention is at least a temporary solution. Thus, the Oral-Rigid finds ways to always be the centre of attention. They may lead a team at work, as this keeps people close. But, if you're in the team, at some point you may develop the feeling that it's all about them. They have to be the star of the show or they will lose interest. They can give a lot of energy to a project but this is done largely to feed their self-image on a regular basis.

As mentioned above, a popular label for these types of behaviours is Narcissism.

Treatment Notes

As mentioned earlier, ideally, we treat the first Safety Strategy, in this case the Oral wound from the mother. However, when working with Compound Structures that feature the Rigid Structure, this is not always practicable.

The Rigid component serves to harden over the Oral wound to the point where the individual is almost certainly in acute denial as to its existence. 'Me, needy? No way!' This may hijack our ability to work directly with the inner sense of need or lack, especially in traditional psychotherapy or anything that seeks to get the client to talk about their inner state.

Body-based techniques can be very handy here. They may be utilised to work on either the Rigid aspect, or to work on the Oral component in a way that bypasses the thinking mind. If we use body-based techniques to dissolve the Rigid armouring only, the risk is that, as soon as the rigidity starts to move, underlying neediness and vulnerability begin to rise, and the client experiences a sudden need to withdraw from therapy.

The ideal way forwards with the Oral-Rigid is to work with the actual expression of anger. Anger is a key component of both the Oral and the Rigid structures. If a client can start to express anger, then both the Oral aspect and the bodily armour characteristic of the Rigid Character will begin to dissipate. Pillow bashing exercises can be great for this, as well as expressing anger face-to-face in a group setting if you are trained in this type of therapy.

However, working directly with anger does also require considerable experience as a therapist. It cannot be done without this. In addition, Oral-Rigid clients may be averse to doing it. In this situation, I recommend deploying separate exercises for the Oral and Rigid aspects.

For the Oral side, belly energy strengthening exercises are great. Also, exercises that evoke blissful infant feelings. Check out the Right-to-Exist, Reichian Belly Breathing and Triple Opener exercises as well as Sucking exercises.

For the Rigid side, deep tissue massage and similar is excellent. Also, exercises that activate the pelvis and the legs and allow these areas to generate spontaneous healing movements for the rest of the body. See more ideas in the section on the Rigid Character Structure too.

Oral – Aggressive

Manifestation

The Oral-Aggressive Character may exist as a slightly different type of narcissist. Instead of binding people to them through manipulation, they focus on creating a dynamic and charismatic front that they can keep up for sufficient time to attract others in.

Understanding

Whilst this Compound Structure may be common in certain classes of stage performers, otherwise I'd say that it is unusual to meet someone with a strong Oral component who is also strong in the Aggressive Structure.

This is because the Oral component is energy-depleting, and the Aggressive Structure needs that egoic drive to run. The Oral-Rigid is far more common because simply creating tension and holding everything in requires less energy and drive.

The Oral-Aggressive type will thus be someone who can become a dynamic ball of energy and charisma for a few days, perhaps for an event they lead, a role they play or to go out on the town. But once this is over, they collapse completely and return to a depressed and needy state, either requiring constant attention or seeking solace in drugs or food.

Treatment Notes

In my opinion, there is actually little that is problematic about the Aggressive Structure, with one big caveat. They need to be sufficiently in touch with their emotions to have a decent level of empathy. Once they can be touched by the events of others' lives, they can invariably put their immense inspirational qualities to good use.

So, following the dictum that we work on the earliest pattern first, it is good to work on the Oral side, whilst still ensuring that the depth of emotion that many Orals are open to does not become cut off.

Oral characters need grounding, likewise Aggressives. So working the circuit from the belly to the soles of the feet is important. Belly Activation and grunting exercises like the Triple Opener or Right-to-Exist are excellent. Exercises that release tension from the leg muscles, such as the Classic Leg Stretch and the Dog-Lion work well. Likewise ankle-opening exercises.

We also want to fill up that gap deep inside the psyche of the Oral Character, where they did not receive the love and connection they expected as an infant. Exercises that make use of the Sucking Reflex are especially helpful to give a sense of deep, inner nourishment.

Enduring Compound Structures

It is very common, especially in Western culture, to find at least some element of the Enduring Character in a person's psyche. It is that part of us that will never fully commit, will never fully go for it, that hangs back wishing to keep his or her options open.

The degree to which we had our natural instinct to express 'no' suppressed as a small child has a big influence on our level of risk aversion and creates a heightened need to feel safe. The huge prevalence of this Enduring trait in our society often creates a back-drop of righteous-sounding outrage at the excesses of individualism. In any crisis, our Endurer side will be there, urging us to hurl blame.

Working on our Enduring side allows us to find the individual within ourselves who has no need for excessive protection, who is emotionally present to feedback and the outcome of his or her behaviour, and who can take responsibility for the risks they take.

Enduring – Rigid

Manifestation

The Enduring-Rigid Character is both afraid to take risks and deeply concerned about their self-image. It's of incredible importance to them that they look good to those around them. They have some of that egoic drive to move forwards, but it is under very careful control, lest they do something that might upset someone or expose them to shame. Their psyche is dominated by guilt.

Old school religious followers embody this Compound Structure. Many in mid-level corporate management do likewise. They love rules and mantras that tell them how to behave and that can be repeated.

They fantasise about getting everything and everyone neatly categorised, and, ideally, barcoded!

Understanding

The voice of the overbearing parent is dominant inside the psyche of this character, forever threatening retribution should they ever dare to step out of the tight behavioural box that they have created for themselves. Rather than suppress their personality entirely, this character has learned to rigidify and control themselves to an extreme degree. Before entering into any social situation, they need to know the 'rules of engagement' – who they should be and how they should behave in order to fit in.

This Compound Character is not cut off from their desires. Rather they are simply terrified to follow them out in the world. They prefer to access the energy of desire in inner fantasy play where no one else can witness or judge them. In some ways, perhaps, the Enduring-Rigid person actually has a worse life than someone who is simply an Endurer. Unlike many Endurers, they know they are cut off from the world because of their rich fantasy life and the fact that it can never be shown to another soul. They are like the kid staring through the shop window, witnessing life but somehow not themselves allowed to enter.

Treatment Notes

The Enduring-Rigid Character is way too dominated by their 'superego' – that internalised voice of authority from Freudian psychoanalysis. This voice has constructed an unbelievably tight behavioural box for them to exist in and left them only with fantasies in which to otherwise express their spontaneity or desire.

The way forward is for them to both begin to articulate to others what it is that they would like to have from life and to take slow steps towards it. Old school behavioural therapy works for them. Learning to progressively take more risks, whilst breathing and feeling the body, will slowly get that nuclear warhead of a superego to stand down. As they are compelled to witness that their fear of social exclusion is ridiculously extreme, that the ground is not going to open up and swallow them whole, so they can begin to enjoy life more.

I recommend 'social challenges' as a good starting point. This can be backed up by emotional expression exercises that work with anger and 'play' exercises that take them back to the childhood world they will have largely missed out on.

Enduring – Aggressive

Manifestation

Now we come to a bizarre character indeed – the Enduring-Aggressive. Like the cartoon character Superman, this Type flits between being mild-mannered and withdrawn to becoming very extroverted and charismatic. The central character in the Jim Carrey movie, The Mask, is another excellent example. This Type may make use of substances, frequently alcohol, to facilitate the change.

Capable of being the life and soul of the party when in the Aggressive phase, nevertheless the next day one meets a withdrawn, meek character whom one can barely credit with their earlier behaviour.

Understanding

The Enduring-Aggressive Character is a personification of the battle between the Freudian Superego and Ego. Mostly, the moralising, guilt-ridden voice of the Superego has control. But once in a while, the Ego gets to come out and play. In the wake of this, up leaps the Superego again, threatening dire consequences and dredging up guilt in its bid to regain control. So it goes around.

Treatment Notes

What is interesting about the Enduring-Aggressive Character is that both aspects need to trust more. The Enduring side needs to trust themselves. The Aggressive side needs to trust the world.

Work slowly on the Enduring side, especially if one is using practices that deliberately evoke anger. Insist that the person spends time introspecting on and speaking about their inner world of thoughts and emotions. They must begin to value their emotional life. This is very important. Add heart-centred exercises and trust exercises too. We want the Enduring side to open up. We want to Aggressive side to do the same.

Rigid Compound Structures

The Rigid personality type is, at its core, simply a holding pattern. We can restrict our exposure to emotionality by holding tight, barricading the feelings in. It leaves us feeling somewhat like a robot, if we can bear to be that honest. It's about control. It's about negotiation. It's about cortical inhibition – our human 'higher mind' taking control of the body.

The issue for the Rigid Character Type is that there is no 'off button.' Although the behaviour of self-restraint and repression happened further down the line than that of the three pre-egoic structures, it has still become written into our bodies. Each morning when we get up, that rigidity in the physical body 'reboots' our minds back into the holding pattern. We cannot just allow life to be, to happen to us. We experience a compulsion to keep it at arm's length, to retain a feeling of control.

The Rigid – Aggressive Type

Manifestation

When I try to bring to my mind's eye the character of the Rigid-Aggressive, I see the successful entrepreneur or business person. Not just a corporate clone. But rather someone who can both follow the rules and go off-track. Driven to both survive and succeed, the Rigid-Aggressive reminds me of one of those 'replicants' in the original Blade Runner movie. Put them down wherever you like on the earth, and they will make the best of it. They will survive, against all odds, and they will thrive, at least in terms of status and personal finance. The Rigid-Aggressive is a survival machine.

Understanding

The Rigid-Aggressive cannot relax. The word has literally no meaning for them. The Rigid side demands that they stay on the hamster wheel, doing something with their mind constantly seeking improvement. The Aggressive side seeks out challenges and competes unrelentingly. Neither side can ever be satisfied with what they have.

Treatment Notes

Whilst the Rigid-Aggressive finds it relatively easy to create an independent and outwardly successful life, filled with material possessions, inside they may still come to suspect that something is nevertheless missing. Perhaps, they see those people who appear to have this thing called 'peace of mind' and it bugs them.

Many in this Structure will likely never get curious in this manner. Their own mind will have pat answers to their occasional inner questions. They will not challenge these and look deeper. But for some, their innate need for risk and self-improvement can save them. They take up the challenge and may seek therapeutic support.

They want to push themselves to allow more vulnerability around others, to be less in control, to show more sides of themselves. For the Rigid-Aggressive, it is all about trusting others, relinquishing control and allowing deeper emotions to be felt and shown. It's a journey. You can't just leap in there. Learning to trust can only be done step by step, feeling your way, constantly checking in.

Any exercise where they have to consciously let go of control will be beneficial. Exercises that increase the felt sense of the back, belly, pelvis, legs and feet are all excellent. The more we feel these areas, the easier it is to feel safe without our mind tightly controlling what's going on.

When the Rigid-Aggressive can allow themselves to deeply weep, and be seen by others in this state, a huge internal barrier will have been surmounted.

Aggressive Compound Structures

All of the possibilities here have already been covered. Still, it's good to be aware of the flight into Aggression that often happens as earlier Structures are worked through. Perhaps we're not yet ready to feel the anger or the pain and so we learn to channel this energy away from our belly and heart and use it to drive ourselves forwards. Perhaps, our formerly pre-egoic pattern was so debilitating that now our natural desire is to just get out into the world and achieve.

Whatever the motivation, do remember that the Aggressive Structure only becomes a problem when our heart is closed.

The Exercises

This chapter will contain clear, concise, illustrated explanations of the postures and workouts referred to in the Exercises sections of this book. I have provided these in alphabetical order.

I recommend practising any exercise you choose to do at least 5 times a week, on separate days, for at least 2 weeks, ideally one month. This time is needed for the body and mind to get into it. Flitting from one exercise to another, in a capricious fashion, is unlikely to achieve anything meaningful. You have to work with this stuff!

Another important point is to find yourself some form of timer that gives a pleasant tone after a length of time that you pre-set. Many of these exercises require that you remain in a posture for a set length of time. If you simply look at a clock or watch, this will take you away from the practice. There are timer apps available online, or I have a series of 'ding tracks,' downloadable from bioenergetics.org.uk.

It is very important that you decide on a length of time that you will do an exercise for in advance, and stick to it, unless it becomes physically painful. Simply having a go at an exercise and stopping when you feel like it is unlikely to achieve anything.

Be aware that you do not need to 'push through' physical pain. If an exercise is physically painful, as opposed to bringing up feelings, then stop. If it is bringing up feelings, then continue to tune into the sense of the body.

You may find bizarre physical effects taking place when you do the exercises. Spasms, contractions, burping, spontaneous shaking and the like are all fairly common. Do your best to allow these things to happen without your mind trying to take control. Your body actually knows just how to release the past without your mind having to do a thing. But, if you do find what's happening to be disturbing, then simply lay off the posture. As ever, tune into the sense of your body.

Before getting into the exercises themselves, it will be useful to describe the two basic body positions used for many of the exercises described in this chapter. Those are the Reichian Working Position and the Grounded Standing Stance. Looking at them first will save a lot of repetition in the descriptions later on! Then we'll go straight into the exercises.

Reichian Working Position

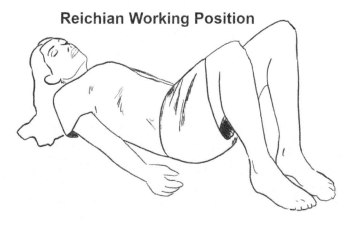

Reichian Working Position

Most of the exercises in this chapter that are done lying down work from this basic posture. It is named after Wilhelm Reich because it was the position that he invariably put clients in when he was working with them.

Lying down on your back on a yoga mat or firm mattress, first ensure that the back of your head is on the mat with your eyes facing toward the ceiling. They may be open or closed. Do not use a pillow unless you have neck issues. Bring the soles of your feet flat on the mat, such that your knees come up, pointing towards the ceiling. Ensure that your heels are a comfortable distance from your ass and that they are about hip-width apart.

That's it! Now you're ready to work.

Grounded Standing Stance

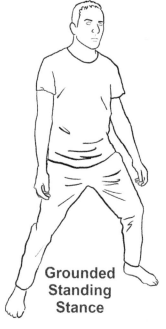

This is the basic position for many Bio-energetics postures. What's particularly important is that you keep your knees at least slightly bent and not locked. People usually begin with bent knees but soon lock through the knees to block feelings. Needless to say, this is not useful.

Stand with your feet either shoulder-width apart or slightly wider. Adjust your feet such that the outsides are roughly parallel. You don't have to make them exactly parallel if this is uncomfortable, but do not have them splayed any more than is necessary. Bend your

Grounded Standing Stance

knees at least slightly and drop your ass a little. Your backbone should be upright, and you should feel some fluidity in your ass, like you could bounce it up and down if you wish. Your neck should also be upright, your eyes open looking straight ahead.

Okay, you've got the Grounded Standing Stance and are ready to work. Remember, keep those knees bent!

Belly Activation Sequence

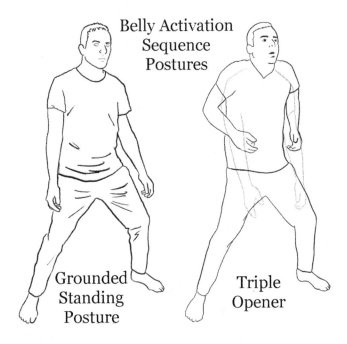

Belly Activation Sequence Postures

Grounded Standing Posture

Triple Opener

This is an excellent set of exercises for progressively bringing more awareness into the belly area, our primate power centre.

Come into the Grounded Standing Stance, see above. Begin the sequence by consciously pushing your belly muscles out to create an inhale, relaxing and then slightly contracting them to exhale. Have your throat relaxed and your mouth slightly open. This is a natural breathing technique for primates, but most humans have learned to breathe with the muscles around the throat and chest, which keeps our fight or flight response triggered. It's tricky at first but do your best to keep your throat simply relaxed and open and drive your breathing consciously from your abdominals. Feel your belly muscles as you expand and relax them. You may have your eyes open or closed as you wish for this stage.

After 5 minutes, we make a slight change. Continue breathing as above, but on the exhale make a low sound, in fact the lowest sound that you can make. It doesn't have to be loud. It shouldn't strain your throat. It's not a chanting sound of any type. The sound should be simply the lowest sound you can make. Continue feeling your belly throughout this stage. Once again, you may keep your eyes open or closed. Ensure that you keep your knees slightly bent.

After 5 minutes of this stage, we come to the final stage – an exercise called the Triple Opener. For this, take your feet wider apart, such that they are now definitely wider than shoulder-width. Do your best to have the outsides of your feet roughly parallel. Keep your knees at least slightly bent. As you inhale, lift your shoulders towards your ears, keeping your arms and hands relaxed. Bring them up as high as they will go. As you exhale, throw your shoulders down with a low grunt sound. Once again, this sound should be the lowest sound you can make. For this stage, as it is more physical and more evocative, you do not need to ensure that you are breathing by using the belly muscles. You just allow your body to breathe however it wishes, keeping your focus on the shoulder movements.

Allow yourself to put any frustration or negativity that you have into the downward movement of the shoulders. Really throw them down as though you are an angry teenager. But do not start screaming and shouting or throwing a tantrum. Just continue with the distinct, low grunt sound. For this stage, keep your eyes open, looking straight ahead. You may find it useful to focus on a point in front of you. Continue this stage for at least 10 minutes, making the downward shoulder movement with a grunt around once a second. There is a 'grunt track' that you can download, to follow along to, listed in the Resources section at the end of this book.

There is a slight variation on this final stage that some people find helps to keep them more grounded. At the same time as you raise your shoulders towards your ears, you also lift your heels off the ground by flexing your toes. Then, when you throw your shoulders down, at the same time you drop your heels back to the floor firmly creating a vibration up your legs.

In addition, the final part of the Belly Activation Sequence – the Triple Opener exercise – can be replaced by the Right-to-Exist exercise to provide some variation. It should be done for the same length of time. Details of this exercise are found later in this chapter.

Belly Breathing

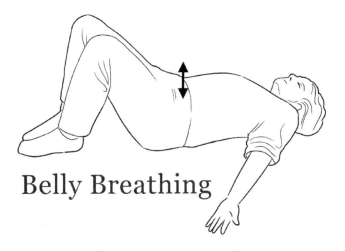

Belly Breathing

Humans have been using the wrong muscles to breathe with, likely for centuries, and it is getting worse. The Western medical world is now confirming this reality. People suffering from conditions like asthma or Chronic Obstructive Pulmonary Disease (OCPD) are routinely taught Abdominal Breathing, a more medically-accurate term for Belly Breathing.

Wilhelm Reich began to write about correct and incorrect breathing nearly a century ago and numerous other physicians, such as Konstantin Buteyko, have also weighed in with their own opinion and developed their own school of thought.

Whether you believe we should breathe only through the nose by abdominal movements, as did Buteyko, or through the mouth with the abdominals and intercostals, as did Reich, one thing is clear. We should not be using the muscles around the neck or throat. These muscles should only be involved in breathing when we require more oxygen, such as in situations where we are facing a threat. Breathing with them on a daily basis keeps our nervous system locked into 'fight or flight mode.'

Corrective action begins by learning and practising Belly Breathing (Abdominal Breathing). Whether we choose to involve the intercostals as well, or whether we choose to breathe through the nose or the mouth, are secondary concerns that needn't trouble us until we've got Belly Breathing down. That's because learning Belly Breathing is so radical, and can create such a level of personal psychological change, that it's not useful to worry about the finer points until we've really got it first.

Let's start practising the technique lying down and then we can move on to standing.

Lie down on your back in the Reichian Working Position (see earlier in this chapter). Now, keeping your mouth slightly open, consciously try to relax your throat, such that the airway from your mouth down into your lungs is like an open channel. Once you feel it is as relaxed as you can get it, you can begin Belly Breathing. Push your abdominals out, ballooning your belly. As you do this, your lungs will be drawn downwards, creating a slight vacuum. If your throat is relaxed and open, air will naturally be drawn in. To create an exhale, relax your abdominals and slightly compress them back in. This movement causes the lungs to be drawn back up, pushing air out. I recommend that when you begin to practise Belly Breathing, you make a relaxed 'Ah' sound on the exhale. This will help to keep you present in your body.

What we're fundamentally doing here is learning to breathe solely with our abdominals, instead of using the muscles around our chest, throat and shoulders. The technique requires that you focus on both your abs, to make sure you are moving them correctly, and on your throat and mouth, to make sure they remain relaxed and open. In addition, because you are consciously creating each breath and thus focussed fully on it, you do not need to leave a gap between the inhale and the exhale. As soon as you complete the inhale, you can start the exhale, and vice versa.

A full cycle of breath, driven from the abs in this way, should take between 5 and 10 seconds. It's no big deal if it's a little longer. But it should not be shorter than 5 seconds. We are not trying to go into hyperventilation.

Continue breathing in this way for at least 10 minutes, remaining focussed primarily on your belly movements, also checking that your throat remains relaxed and your mouth slightly open. When you are able to 'entrain' your mind to this technique and stay present with it, you will have learned Belly Breathing, lying down.

Doing it over time, you may experience all manner of spontaneous tremblings, contractions, muscle spasms and similar. This is all good and to be expected. Simply allow anything that is truly spontaneous, and coming from the body, to just happen. Do not try to 'move things along' in any way! Your body knows how to unlock itself without any input from your thinking mind.

The technique can also be practised whilst sitting, kneeling or standing. Although it tends not to go so deep in this way, it is nevertheless useful, especially as a component of a series of Bioenergetic exercises.

Either sit, kneel or get in the Grounded Standing Stance. Now, as when you were lying down, just push your abdominals out to create an in-breath, keeping your throat relaxed and your mouth slightly open. Allow your abs to relax and then contract them slightly to exhale.

As you work with Belly Breathing over time, it's a good practice to focus especially on the lower abdominals and ensure that you are really involving these muscles in the breathing process.

Belly Breathing Sitting Meditation

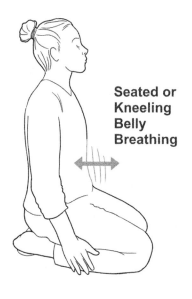

Seated or Kneeling Belly Breathing

In addition to doing Belly Breathing lying down or standing, it can also be a truly excellent technique to practice sitting. Done this way, it's very similar to the original version of Vipassana Meditation, the first meditation practice given by The Buddha after his enlightenment, some 2,500 years ago.

Find a comfortable way to sit or kneel. If you are sitting on a chair, please just ensure that the soles of your feet can be flat on the floor. With eyes closed, begin the Belly Breathing technique described above. The only difference is that, this time, we are going to have our mouths gently closed, so that air can naturally flow in and out through the nose.

So, with your throat as relaxed as you can make it, balloon your belly out, particularly your lower abdomen, drawing your lungs down and creating an inhale. As soon as the belly movement has gone as far as it can, begin to reverse, relaxing the abdominals and then slightly contracting them as well. Continue with this cycle, ensuring that a full cycle of breath takes at least 5 seconds, no shorter.

Try to gently concentrate your attention on the movements your belly is making. The phrase 'gently concentrate' might seem strange, but it just means to focus here without making your face or upper body tense. If you're successful at focusing in this manner, you will find after a few minutes that you have become naturally entrained to the movements of your belly and that you can stay like this without too much effort. You will have entered a state of meditation.

Try to perform this practice for 10 minutes initially and work up to 20 minutes as you become experienced.

This type of meditation, when you have got the hang of it, can create huge inner transformation. You will find yourself progressively more centred at the belly and, as this happens, your upper body can relax and open more.

The Bow & Arch

Arch

Bow

The Bow and Arch postures are one of the cornerstone practises in Bioenergetics. They are actually useful for all five of the Character Structures, as well as being an excellent daily workout to maintain a grounded openness. The Bow is one stretch and the Arch is its counter-stretch.

To begin the Bow posture, stand with your feet shoulder-width apart and with the outsides of your feet roughly parallel. Have your knees slightly bent such that your legs aren't locked straight. Look straight ahead. Bring your arms up above your head, stretched fully and with palms facing forwards.

Now, bring your stretched arms back behind your ears and, at the same time, press your pelvis forwards. Keep your neck upright, with eyes open, looking straight ahead. This will bring your body roughly into the shape of an archer's bow, hence the name of the posture. Maintaining this stretch, breathe and feel your body.

Bioenergetics, unlike some bodywork practices, is not all about the posture. The posture is just one of three elements. The others are breathing and feeling. If you're focusing totally on the posture, and not paying attention to your breath and the sense of your body, then you are not doing it! So, do your best to breathe with your belly, as in the Belly Breathing description above, and try to stay tuned in to the sense of your body.

With the Bow posture, it is actually not so important that your body looks like the illustration. Rather it's important that you are pushing in the right places. Stretch your arms back, so that you feel the compression in the area of the shoulder blades. Gently push your pelvis forwards. In addition, try to keep your chest open, by keeping your shoulders back. Don't allow them to 'close' in front of your chest. Also, keep your knees slightly bent and most definitely not locked straight.

If you are one of those people who is quite flexible in the mid-back, you may be capable of stretching your upper body a long way back. This is actually not needed in the Bow posture. You only need to go as far back as in the illustration.

The counter-stretch to the Bow is the Arch. Come out of the Bow by gently lowering your arms and straightening your body. Once you're back standing upright, then start the Arch by lowering your chin to your chest. Once it's travelled as far as it can, continue to slowly hang forwards until either you've gone as far as you can or your fingertips are just off the floor. If you're quite flexible then you don't need to go down so far that you touch the floor.

Now that you're hanging in the correct position, pay attention to the following three points of the posture, whilst still breathing nice and deep and remaining present with the sense of your body:

- Give your head and arms a little jiggle periodically, just to check that you are not locking at the neck or shoulders. These parts of your body should feel loose, rather like a rag-doll.

- Straighten through the legs, as though your tail-bone is being pulled upwards, but keep a tiny bit of flex left in your knees.

- Take your weight slightly more towards your toes than your heels. Your heels should remain in contact with the floor.

If the Arch posture feels like it might be too much for your lower back, then take the weight off by placing your hands or your elbows on your knees for a while, whilst continuing to breathe deeply and feel your body.

When you come out of the Arch position, come out slowly. It should feel like you're uncurling, vertebrae by vertebrae. Your head comes up last. Try to remain feeling the body as you come out.

This pair of postures can be practised one after the other for multiple sets. I recommend you start with 3 sets. That's to say you do the Bow for a specific time, then come into the Arch, then back to the Bow, continuing until you've done three of each.

As to the length of time you should remain in each posture, I recommend that you start with 1 minute. If that feels too much, reduce it. If it's easy, increase the length of time on your dinging app.

Cervical 'Despair Release' Exercise

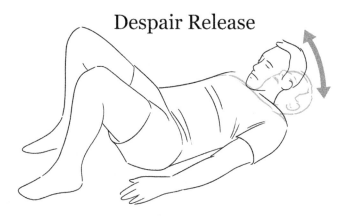

Despair Release

This exercise is drawn from Reichian Therapy and works the Cervical Armour Segment – a ring of muscular tension that accumulates around the neck and throat. It is done in the Reichian Working Position. You will need a mattress to lie on that is sufficiently soft that, when lying on your back with your head raised, you can let your head fall back and it isn't painful.

Lie down on your back with your knees up and the soles of your feet planted. Your feet should be hip-width apart. Before beginning the exercise, practice Belly Breathing for a few minutes.

This exercise is a development of the 'Cry Breathing' technique that will be covered later in this chapter. You break the in-breath up into 6-8 distinct short inhales through the mouth, in the manner of a young child breathing histrionically to protest about something they don't want to do. If you try it, you should recognise this type of breath from your childhood. As you perform the in-breath, you simultaneously raise your head as far as it will go, whilst keeping your shoulders still on the mattress.

When your head is fully raised, and you've completed this broken up in-breath, you breathe out with an 'Ah' sound whilst letting your head simply fall back to the mattress. It's important to neither control this falling back movement of the head, nor the expression of the 'Ah' sound. Just let go, as though giving up trying to control the situation. This aspect of the exercise is vital. If you try to control the let-go, the exercise will not work.

Once your head is back down and you have fully exhaled, take 3 or 4 Belly Breaths to integrate, then perform the 'Despair Release' breath again and continue in this manner. Once you've completed your allotted time, stretch your legs out and relax totally, still feeling your body, for at least 3 minutes.

You may do this exercise either with eyes open or closed. I recommend that you perform this exercise for 5 minutes and see how you feel afterwards. Feel free to work up to 20 minutes.

Chest Ring Armour Release

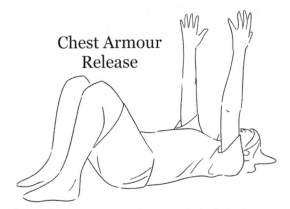

Chest Armour
Release

This exercise works on the ring of armour identified by Reich as being below the Cervical layer and above the Diaphragmatic – the Chest Ring. When we feel open in the chest, we can allow human emotions to flow within us more deeply and without having to employ some form of avoidance strategy to reduce our exposure to them.

We begin lying on the mat in the Reichian Working Position (see explanation of this posture at the beginning of this chapter). Start Belly Breathing for several minutes until, hopefully, your mind has become entrained to it, and you don't have to focus too hard.

Now, reach up with both arms, keeping your palms facing and shoulder width apart. Really stretch your arms up, such that your shoulders come off the mat. Keep your eyes open and focus on a point on the ceiling above you. Begin saying the word "please" in the language you spoke as a child, as though you are begging for something from someone above you.

Do your best to free associate from this "please" word. This means actually speaking out what simply arises uncensored in your mind. It might sound like:

- Please help me, Dad. I need you to support me. I don't understand what's going on. Where are you?

- Please see me, Mom. Stop being busy. Please give it to me. I need your attention.

The above are just examples from my own mind. Do your best to not censor what is there and just allow yourself to vocalise. This will be easier if you know no one is around who could hear you. Speaking actual words and phrases that are coming from inside of you will increase the level of energetic movement and emotional release from the ring of chest armour in this exercise.

One tip with free association is to always say something. Even if there is just nothing there, say 'there's nothing there' and continue speaking and stuff will just come. This is how the mind works.

I recommend that you do this exercise to a ding track, initially set for

1 minute. For the first minute, practice Belly Breathing with your arms by your side. Then reach up and free associate on "please" for 1 minute. Repeat these two steps three times and then allow yourself to stretch out fully and relax for 5 minutes at the end to give yourself some processing and integration time.

Once you are experienced with this exercise, feel free to change the 'seed word' that is used to begin free association. Here are some suggestions for words or phrases that most people will find evocative:

- Give it to me!
- I want…
- I need…
- No!
- Yes!

Croak Breathing

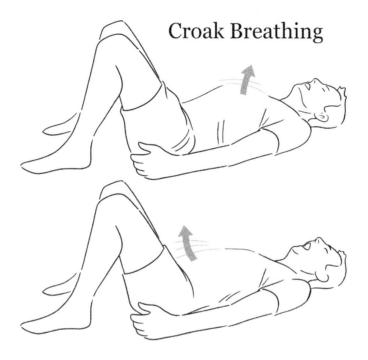

Croak Breathing

This Reichian breathing technique is excellent for breaking up armour in the diaphragm area. However, it is quite an advanced technique and you will need to have mastered Belly Breathing and Rapid Inhale Belly Breathing before attempting it.

Lie down on your mat in the Reichian Working Position (see beginning of chapter for description). I'll describe the exact technique as bullet points, as it's a little complex:

- Having fully exhaled, perform a partial inhale to the chest area only. This should be roughly half a full chest inhale. Perform this inhale abruptly and with a short 'croak' sound. This sound should be like one of the inhalations of a dying man, sometimes known as a 'death rattle.' The inhale and croak should last no longer than one second.

- Hold that partial inhale for a very short period, perhaps around a half second.

- Now perform a rapid upward flick of the abdominals and then exhale slowly with an "Ah" sound. A fuller description of this upward flick of the abs is found later in this chapter as 'Rapid Inhale Belly Breathing.'

- When fully exhaled, start again.

When done correctly, this powerful technique can begin to clear rigidity and energetic blockages in the area of the diaphragm. Once you can feel your diaphragm moving whilst breathing normally, there will be a far greater sense of freedom and sensuality in your life.

I recommend that, before getting too deeply into this exercise, you do slowly go through it to make sure that you really have it down. It is a little complex at first. If you check my YouTube channel, you should also find a video on 'Croak Breathing.'

Once you are confident that you are doing the technique correctly, I recommend you begin practising it for just 1 or 2 minutes, gradually working your way up to 20 to 30 minutes.

Also note that, once proficient, Croak Breathing can accelerate the release of armour rings around the head and throat area when combined with specific techniques for those areas.

Cry Breathing

Cry Breathing is another excellent Reichian technique for creating a release in the lateral rings of armour that bind the trunk of the body in an unhealthy manner. What I also love about this method is that it is based on a way of breathing that pretty much all of us will have indulged in as kids.

At around the age of two most of us begin to create our own ego – our sense of personal selfhood. The way that this usually manifests is by us screaming and shouting "no" and generally protesting about things that our parents, or other caregivers, want us to do. Our mum takes us to the supermarket with her and we just scream and scream the whole time. Our dad perhaps leaves us sitting in the back of the car while he talks to a friend and we do the same.

As we advance in years a little more, this simple screaming evolves into a form of histrionic demonstration known here as 'Cry Breathing.' We are not really in pain when our parents take us on a car journey that we don't want to go on. But we mimic deep wounding by breathing in a specific manner as a form of protest.

We break up the in-breath into 6-8 quite noisy short inhales and then we exhale in one go with a similarly dramatic noise, as though suffering deeply. Give it a try or look for a video on the technique on my YouTube channel. I'm sure you will recognise this pattern of breathing once you get it.

Performing Cry Breathing as an adult can help us to release self-pity and a complaining attitude. It helps us to take responsibility for our own life and to be an adult. I recommend you practice it lying down in the Reichian Working Position described at the beginning of this chapter. From fully exhaled, perform at least 6 micro-inhales with some level of sound, until full. Then exhale in one drawn out gasp, as though suffering.

Perform the exercise initially for at least 5 minutes, feeling your body closely whilst doing so. Feel free to work up to 20 or 30 minutes. Like many of these Reichian breath techniques, it can take a while to both get it and to move through resistance to doing it. But once this is done, it can go very deep.

Crying Exercise

This is not a complicated exercise. All you do is literally try to make yourself feel sad, and cry. Our minds often make feeling and expressing emotions a very complicated business. But actually emotions are quite autonomic and should come naturally when we encounter certain outer or inner situations. But, growing up, we may have learned to suppress tears and the accompanying feeling of vulnerability to feel safer and more in control of our lives.

If we go through the physical and mental motions of inducing sadness and tears, in an emotionally healthy person they will come. So that is what we practice in this exercise.

Sitting down in a comfortable position, call to your mind any event which makes you sad. At the same time, let your face and the rest of your body adopt a position that you associate with sadness and crying. Perhaps you slightly screw your face up and have your hands open to suggest powerlessness. Experiment for yourself. You may also wish to put on some evocative music.

Once you've started, allow your body to shudder as though racked by sadness. Keep feeling inside and see if tears come.

I recommend you try this exercise initially for 5 minutes and that you do use music. Feel free to work up from there as you wish.

Deep Neck Release Sequence

Oral Characters, in particular, often have a neck that cranes forwards, as though trying to reach the nipple or another source of nourishment. This brief sequence of exercises can be very useful for creating a rapid release of some of the tension which holds a neck like this in its unnatural position.

Each of the postures works by increasing neck tension to an extreme for a few seconds, followed by a physical movement and expression of sound. So you will need to do this exercise in an environment where you feel okay to make a reasonably loud shouting sound a few times. Once the four different neck release postures are complete, we lie down in a specific position to relax and integrate the release.

Stand in the Grounded Standing Stance described at the beginning of this chapter.

Neck Release 1 & 2: Bring the palm of your left hand to the left side of your head with your left elbow pointing to the side and your fingers pointing behind you. Place your palm just forward of your ear, as shown in the illustration. Now, for a few seconds, push your head to the right with all your

Neck Release Sequence

might, whilst simultaneously resisting movement with your neck muscles. We are trying to briefly create maximum tension in specific neck muscles. There should be no overall movement, merely a sensation of huge tension. When you have created the maximum tension possible for a few seconds, release the position by hurling your arm downwards and making a spontaneous sound. After a brief period, repeat the exercise, this time with the right hand on the right side of the head.

Neck Release 3: This time take both palms and place them on your forehead, with your elbows pointing forwards and your fingers pointing up. Now, push your head back and, like before, resist the movement by creating tension in your neck muscles. As before, when you've created the maximum tension possible in your head and neck for a few seconds, quickly release the position by throwing your arms down and making a sound.

Neck Release 4: This is the big one! Take both hands and, interlinking your fingers, place them right at the back of your head, around the occipital point. Bring your elbows to the front. Pull your head forwards with all your might, at the same time resisting any movement by tensing your neck muscles. Release in the same way as before.

Devavani Child Gibberish

The phrase 'Devavani' means 'spirit voice' in Sanskrit and this gentle exercise is drawn from the work of the latter-day Indian mystic, Osho, who created a meditation based around it. Even though it may seem silly, it can go very deep.

Beginning from sitting comfortably on the floor, start to make pre-verbal child sounds – 'goo-goo gah-gah,' and the like. Allow your mind to simply continue, exploring the infant state before we began to develop proper language. If you find this difficult, be aware that you are likely quite deep in the Rigid Strategy and almost certainly have a strong, controlling mind. If so, try to persist until you find it easy to make this preverbal, infant gibberish.

Whilst you make the sound, try to remain feeling your body. Allow yourself to roll around and lie or crawl around the floor, infant-like. But do not come up to standing or do anything else preverbal infants wouldn't do. Continue for 10 – 20 minutes, simply exploring the sounds, the movements and the sense of the body whilst doing them. To complete, lie flat out on the floor for at least five minutes, remaining tuned in to the felt sense of the body.

Dragon's Breath Exercise

Dragon's
Breath

This famous old exercise from the annals of body-based therapy is a great way to open up the throat and experience some release.

Stand with your feet considerably wider than shoulder-width apart. Check that your feet are not excessively splayed in this position, that your knees are bent and that your ass is dropped. Keep your backbone upright.

Imagine that you are a big, angry dragon and that you are not in a good mood! Bring your arms to the front, as in the illustration, as though they are your dragon wings. Now, in one movement perform the following:

- Bring your arms back as far as they will easily travel

- Crane your neck forwards

- Stick your tongue out, and down towards your chin, as far as it will go

- Make a deep hissing sound of disgust from your throat, rather as though you are vomiting on the world

- Make your eyes into horizontal slits, look angry and imagine yourself spitting fire

This should all take a couple of seconds and then you return to the starting position with your arms forwards and your neck back upright.

I recommend that you perform this movement about ten times in a row, allowing a break of about five seconds between each one. It may make you need to spit or cough, so have some tissue handy. The main part where people get it wrong is to not really stick their tongue out and down. It should be stretched out as far as you can.

Eye Rotation Exercise

A curious aspect of body-based therapy is that there are a few areas of the body that seem to reach really deep into our psyche. Even small amounts of movement here have the potential to create deep change. The throat is one and the eyes are another.

Eye Rotation

Simply moving our eyeballs around in a certain fashion has been found to both dig up all sorts of repressed memories and cause pulsations of feeling in the body. Nowadays, there is even a whole therapeutic modality – Eye Movement Desensitisation & Reprocessing (EMDR) – that makes use of this effect.

This exercise can either be done sitting or lying down on your back. Whichever you choose, you should be comfortable.

Doing your best to not move your head, simply rotate your gaze in the widest circle you can make. Continue in one direction for 1 minute and then reverse direction for the same length of time. Do not rotate your gaze so fast that it just becomes a blur. You should be able to take in, at least briefly, everything you see. Also, do your best to remain feeling your body whilst your gaze is rotating. If you can perform belly breathing whilst doing it, this is also great, but not vitally important.

I recommend that you perform a minute of rotations one way, then the other, then close your eyes and feel your body for 1 minute. Perform three repetitions of this sequence. Be aware that, even though this exercise isn't very physical, it nevertheless can dredge up all sorts of old memories and feelings. Pay attention to your mental state for the rest of the day.

Forehead Ring Armour Release

Forehead Armour Release

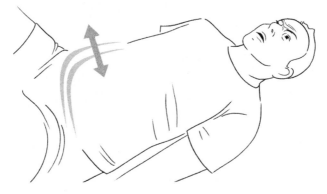

The area of our forehead appears to be one of the main areas in which tension is stored in us higher primates. Our characteristically large frontal lobes and prefrontal cortex give us humans phenomenal powers of thinking. They enable us to model, think and plan conceptually. Combined with directive action, these powers enable us to change our environment on a scale no other animal can begin to approach.

However, if we spend our lives only thinking, and not being in touch with our feelings or our sense of the body then eventually we feel stale, robotic and disconnected. The issue is not thinking itself. But rather the areas of physical tension that accumulate as a result of excessive thinking and that serve to keep us 'stuck in the head,' unable to easily switch off and return to the sensational world. The forehead is one of those areas. So, learning how to work the lateral ring of tension around the forehead is very useful.

Lying down on a mat in our Reichian Working Position, begin by practising Belly Breathing for 4 minutes (see description earlier). Then, keeping your eyes open, attempt to furrow your brow to the max, creating the deepest grooves you can. Try to hold your brow in this state of tension for another 4 minutes, whilst continuing to breathe with your abdominals as before.

Practising this exercise, like many of the Reichian breathing and armour release exercises, you may find weird sensations, spasms, contraction or shakings starting to happen. Just allow anything that's happening spontaneously to happen and keep feeling your body.

Feel free to extend the furrowing part of this exercise up to 10 minutes or longer. The trickiest part is to keep your brow fully furrowed, even while exhaling. We tend to naturally release a bit on the out-breath, so pay particular attention and keep your brow fully furrowed all the time to get the release.

Free Writing Exercise

Whilst not strictly Bioenergetics or Reichian Therapy, this popular exercise can nevertheless prove very liberating and may help whenever a block in more physical process work seems to have been reached.

Before beginning, do something to loosen yourself up a bit. I recommend the Kundalini Shaking exercise described later in this chapter. Do it for at least 5 minutes. Then, sit down with a pen and paper and begin simply writing. Start with a sentence and just continue. The challenge is to allow yourself to express without censoring, to simply 'get out of the way' and allow your mind to unload. Write for either a preset time, I recommend 10 minutes, or for a set number of pages, I recommend three. Then get up and begin the Kundalini Shaking again for another five minutes, really ensuring that you are breathing out deeply through the mouth. To complete the exercise, destroy the paper without reading it.

Get Off My Back – Legs Exercise

Get Off My Back (legs)

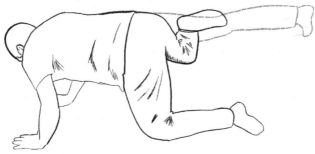

Pretty much all of us carry around this sense of there being someone on our back, monitoring our behaviour and criticising us. In the early days of psychology, this controlling presence was known as the Superego – an internalised voice of authority with the role of keeping our behaviour within societal norms. Often the voice is coming from our parents, or other caregivers, frequently mixed with the social principles we picked up in our formative years.

There's nothing so wrong with this inner voice. We do need some level of self-control, especially in our developmental years. But for many it can become excessively restrictive. It's critical and controlling presence serves to block us from adequately exploring life's myriad possibilities and finding out who we are. This exercise, and the one that follows it, are designed to create a level of physical release from the specific muscles where this 'superego tension' accumulates.

Come to kneeling, in the 'table-top' position, on your mat. Ensure that there is nothing close behind you and that you're in an environment where you can make a reasonable level of noise. Practice kicking backwards, and slightly up, a couple of times, with each leg, such that you can gauge how much force you can comfortably put into kicks like this.

Now, begin kicking backwards and slightly up with one leg after the other. Make the kicks deliberate actions and as you perform them, say the words "Get off my back!" with force. Ideally, time the word "back" to coincide with the final bit of the kick. Feel free to free-associate and swear as you progress with this. See what situations from the past and language spontaneously come up as you continue.

Continue for 1 to 2 minutes, or until you feel some form of cathartic release has occurred. Then, to relax and integrate, bring your ass back to your heels and lean forwards into the Child Pose from yoga.

Get Off My Back Shoulder Exercise

Get Off My Back
(elbows)

This is the version of the previous exercise for the shoulders. It can release surprisingly deep layers of tension from around the shoulder-blades and neck.

Kneeling on your mat, this time with your back upright, you are going to dig back with your elbows, one after the other, as though there literally is someone on your back. Give a few practice digs, such that you can assess how much energy you can give this exercise without risking hurting yourself.

Now begin, once again speaking aloud the phrase "Get off my back!" in time with the digs. Use one elbow after the other. Don't get too mechanical with it. Keep it vital and in the moment. Your upper body should not twist. The movement is from the shoulders. Free-associate and use swear words. See what comes up from your past spontaneously. After a few minutes, or when you feel complete, lean forwards into the Child Pose to relax and integrate.

Gibberish

Speaking a language of your own, that no one else can understand, might seem like a pretty dumb thing to do! But it has immense psychological value for a simple reason. Our habitual use of normal language tends to restrain emotionality when it should actually facilitate it.

When we speak, feelings should come up naturally as our mind constructs narratives about what's happening in our life. You may have even noticed that something unprocessed from your recent past can exert a kind of 'gravitational pull' on your conversation. Like we're trying consciously to not go into the feeling it created but somehow the topic seems to keep coming up!

The therapeutic technique of Gibberish makes use of this principle. The idea is that you simply walk around speaking an utterly incomprehensible language of your own creation. Try to allow it to simply come. There is a part of the brain that can do this easily, when it's activity is not being consciously repressed. (That repression, when it happens, is to keep the underlying feelings suppressed, of course.) As you gibber, allow your body to also be involved. Move your arms around, Latino-style, and let your whole body express the sentiment coming up in the gibbering.

It is an acquired technique. If you find it difficult to get into, then just keep practising. But also don't just go into judgements and make the process 'wrong' in some way. If it's a struggle, then that will be because your level of self-censorship is high.

Gibber for at least 10 minutes and endeavour to keep feeling your body whilst you're doing it. As you let go of conscious censorship, you will notice that sensations and emotions being held beneath the surface naturally come up and simply allowing that creates processing. Complete by spending some time relaxing, simply feeling your body.

Grounding Through the Legs Sequence

This is a powerful set of exercises to open up varying groups of muscles in the legs. This supports the channel from the belly to the soles of the feet to open, such that we feel more present on the earth, more grounded. It's a sequence of 6 exercises that flow into each other and that are usually performed on a 60 second ding. There's a rest exercise that comes at the end of the sequence, before you begin the next rep. Three reps are good, meaning this workout will take a total of 21 minutes.

You'll need a yoga mat that you can roll out, butting one of the short sides up to a bare stretch of wall.

Begin by standing on your mat with your back to the wall. With the first ding, begin moving through the following sequence of postures, doing your best to remain feeling your body the whole time:

1) Lean forwards into the Arch posture; see description earlier in this chapter.

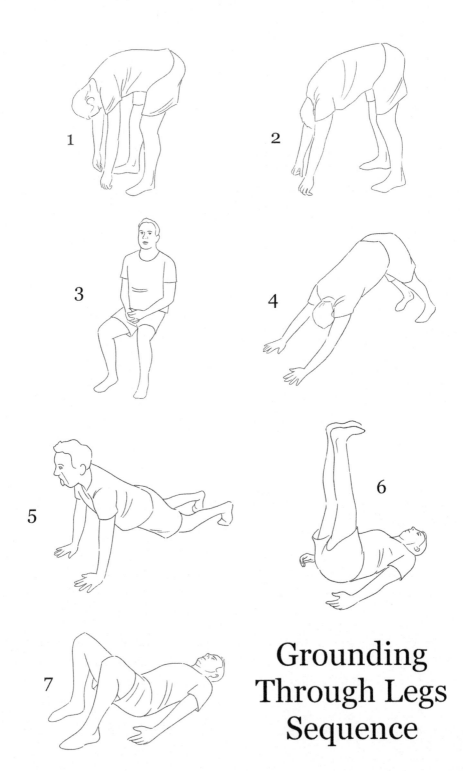

Grounding
Through Legs
Sequence

2) At the ding, lean further forwards, bringing your hands to the floor and resting your weight on the middle knuckles of your hands while straightening your legs.

3) At the ding, bend your knees and, without coming fully up, sit back against the wall behind you. If you begin the sequence at the right distance from the wall this is easier.

4) At the ding, again without coming right up, push out from the wall and lean forwards, coming into the Dog posture from yoga.

5) At the ding, and keeping your weight solely on your palms and the balls of your feet, drop your crotch, straighten your legs and come into the Lion pose. During the minute, periodically open your mouth, stick your tongue out and roar.

6) At the ding, drop your knees to the mat and roll over onto your back. With your back on the mat, bring your straightened legs up at ninety degrees to the trunk of your body. Straighten through the knees as much as you can, whilst breathing and feeling your body.

7) At the ding, bring your legs down and stretch right out, eyes closed, simply relaxing and feeling your body. This is the rest phase.

8) Begin the next rep of the sequence.

"I feel..." Mirror Exercise

"I feel" Mirror
Exercise

Working with the reflection of the face has always comprised a significant element of Reichian Therapy and Bioenergetics. For this exercise, and the one that follows, I recommend that you use a wardrobe mirror or similar free-standing three-quarter-length mirror.

Sitting comfortably in front of the mirror, spend a couple of minutes simply looking at your face, taking yourself in. Endeavour to simply be with how you are, not trying to change anything. Now begin a free association exercise, speaking to yourself in the mirror. Start your sentence with "I feel..." and allow yourself to fill in the words uncensored. Explore with your mind what comes up, all the time trying to breathe in a deep and relaxed manner. Stay present with the sense of your body as you speak.

Continue for between ten and thirty minutes and then lie down and relax for 5 minutes, remaining feeling your body.

"I Need To Love" Mirror Exercise

This is another free association exercise, similar to the one above, but perhaps more emotionally evocative. Once again, sit comfortably in front of your mirror and spend some minutes simply taking in your face, not trying to change anything. When ready, begin to say the words, "I need to love," free-associating with whatever comes up naturally in their wake. Do your best to allow any emotions that come up. Continue for 10 to 30 minutes and then relax, lying flat out with your eyes closed.

Kick-Out Grounding

Kick Out Grounding

This Reichian exercise works the legs, helping to release holding patterns from those muscles that do so much work for us. You will need to do it on a fairly firm bed mattress.

Lying down on your back on the mattress with your legs stretched out straight, begin to lift your legs, one after the other, and bring them down quite firmly on the mattress. Keep your legs straight through the knees. This is very important. I recommend that, to begin, you lift each leg to a height of roughly one foot (30 cm) and that you do about one downward kick each second.

After a couple of minutes of doing the exercise like this, you may find a natural speed and height of kick happening spontaneously, rather as though your legs and pelvis are taking over. If this happens, allow it, and let your mind sit back and give over the sense of control to the legs. If it's not happening, then simply continue kicking at the original pace and height, all the time doing your best to simply feel your legs.

This simple exercise is often very powerful when done for up to 60 minutes at a time. It can create an incredible sense of grounding. Remember to keep your legs as straight as you can! To complete, simply lie flat out relaxing.

Kneeling Trust Fall Exercise

Kneeling
Trust Fall

This simple and interesting little exercise can have a surprisingly deep effect on some people. It's done from standing and before you begin it, I recommend doing a few reps of the Bow & Arch, to create a sense of openness in your body. You will need a firm cushion to come down onto.

Having done a few reps of Bow & Arch, come to standing with your knees slightly bent. Have the firm cushion in front of you on the floor. Now, slowly begin to bend your legs, until you can no longer control your descent, and you fall forwards with your knees onto the cushion. Allow your upper body to follow the movement, such that it comes to the floor in no specific position. Before beginning, obviously ensure that the floor has sufficient cushioning such that you are not going to hurt yourself.

The objective is to find that spot, as you bend your knees, where you have to let go of mental control and trust gravity. Then, when you've reached it, simply allow your body to fall without trying to control the descent. Therefore, do this exercise slowly and with awareness. When you've done it a few times, and had the experience of letting go of control, simply lie down and feel your body to integrate.

Kundalini Shaking

Allowing your body to shake up and down is a powerful technique to both stimulate and relax. It has even become a religious practice in Indonesia. To work effectively, it needs to be done in a specific manner.

Ancient Hindus believed in the presence of a healing, spiritual energy in the body, named *kundalini*, that needed to be awakened, serpent-like, from its base in the region of the ass. Shaking the body in a specific way was believed to achieve this.

Stand upright with your knees slightly bent

Kundalini
Shaking

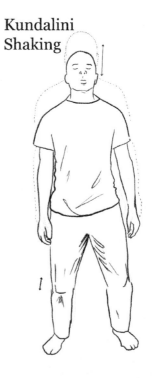

and your feet about shoulder-width apart. You may have your eyes open or closed. But, obviously, open them if you should feel unstable at any point. Feel into your legs and try to begin a subtle, vertical trembling, rather like an animal shaking after a scary encounter. Whether it feels natural or forced, allow this shaking to propagate upwards, until your whole body is shaking vertically.

Pay special attention to your neck, as this is an area that many people lock tight when beginning to shake. It should be loose, such that your head can simply bob up and down as though it were just another part of your body.

Breathe out deeply through the mouth, making a gentle "huh" sound. This is very important. Beginning a vertical shake, many people will lock their throat muscles subconsciously, to try and maintain control. Breathing out deeply with sound stops this from happening.

I recommend you shake initially for 10 minutes. You can work up to one or two hours. As well as being a practice in its own right, doing Kundalini Shaking is also a great way to relax and integrate at the end of other exercises.

Kung Fu Punching with Sound

Kung Fu Punching with Sound

Though more of a martial arts practice, this technique can be great for centring and bringing more feeling into the belly area.

Stand upright, with your feet wide apart and knees bent, backbone vertical. Make tight fists and bring both arms back, such that your elbows point backwards and your fists are in line with your waist. Your fingers should be uppermost in your closed fists. Now, punch forwards with one fist, twisting it through 180 degrees as you do so and making the sound "Hoo" as the punch completes. Then, reversing that punch back to the start position, simultaneously punch forwards with the other fist in the same manner. Try to engage your belly muscles in the movement. Continue like this for several minutes.

Laughing Exercise

The physical exercise of laughing is actually a powerful Bioenergetic exercise. When we laugh, we use a lot of the muscles that are associated with repressing feelings so it's an intrinsically healthy practice. This is especially true of belly laughing.

Sit down in a comfortable position, whether on a chair, cushion or the floor and simply begin to laugh. Try to make a deep sound, as much as possible from the belly, rather like a Santa Claus, Ho-ho-ho type laugh. Continue for 5 minutes. If there are times when you find yourself judging this forced laughing as 'fake,' do not stop because of this. Simply continue laughing. To complete the exercise, lie down on your back with your eyes closed and feel your body. Feel free to perform this exercise for up to an hour or more.

Mirror Affirmation Exercise

The Enduring type Character in particular needs to develop a sense of value for his or her own feelings and inner world. They learned as a child not to attribute worth to these aspects of their life and this exercise is a great way to change that.

Standing in front of a mirror, say ten times out loud the sentence "I value my feelings," paying attention to your face and the feeling of your body while you do so. This exercise should be done daily, shortly after waking for a period of at least a month.

Ocular Ring Armour Release

Ocular Armour Release

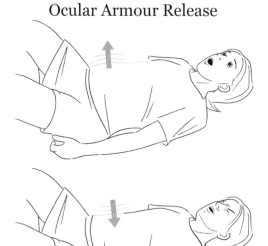

Wilhelm Reich first described the presence of a lateral ring of muscular tension around the eyes back in the 1930s. It's particularly present in those who have tendencies to dissociate – those who utilise the Leaving Strategy.

Lying down in the Reichian Working Position, begin by practising Belly Breathing for several minutes. When ready, begin the exercise by opening and closing your eyes in time with your breathing. As you inhale with your abdominals, open your eyes as wide as you can. As you exhale, close your eyes as tightly as possible. Continue for 5 minutes. Practice staying really present in your body, feeling what's going on. This is especially important with this exercise as it is highly evocative and many will find themselves rapidly drifting off somewhere in their mind.

Oral Ring Armour Release

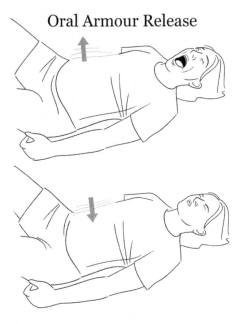

Oral Armour Release

This exercise works on the layer of Reichian armour immediately beneath that worked in the last exercise – around the mouth. It is very similar in concept.

Lying down, in the Reichian Working Position, first begin Belly Breathing for a few minutes. When ready, begin to open and close your mouth in time with your breathing. On the inhale, done entirely from the abs, open your mouth as wide as you can. On the exhale, close it tightly. Continue for 5 minutes, really paying attention to the sensation of your body as you do.

Parent-Child Eye Exercise

This simple eye movement exercise makes use of the fact that, as children, we habitually looked up to pay attention to our parents and that, as adults, we habitually looked down to pay attention to our kids. These actions, of looking down or looking up, have thus over time come to have some degree of psychological significance in the area of dominant or submissive behaviour. This is also reflected in our common use of terms such as 'looking up to someone' or 'looking down on someone.'

The exercise is usually done sitting or kneeling in a comfortable position. Begin by performing Belly Breathing for several minutes. When ready to begin, keeping your head level, simply turn your gaze upwards as though trying to pay attention to someone considerably taller than you. I recommend that you do this exercise facing a wall and put a mark on the wall at a suitable height such that your gaze will be stretched. Continue Belly Breathing whilst gazing up, trying as much as you can to not move your actual head in any way.

After 2 minutes, return to gazing straight ahead, Belly Breathing for another 2 minutes. Then, again keeping your head level, turn your gaze down as though paying attention to someone lower than you. I recommend placing a mark on the floor to help you to remain focused. Continue this for 2 minutes also, again Belly Breathing throughout. Then return to the centre position.

It generally works well to perform two or three reps of this exercise and then to give yourself some integration time either sitting or lying down relaxing.

If you have a friend or partner who is interested in this work, you may do this exercise together, taking turns to play the child or parent role. One stands, whilst the other sits in front of them, gazing at each other. Then rest for a few minutes and reverse roles.

However, if you choose to do this, please be aware that this exercise can be very evocative. So do take time to come out of the parent and child roles at the end. Give each other a hug whilst saying "Thank you for supporting me" and perhaps take time to share one-to-one about your experience.

Pelvic Activation Sequence

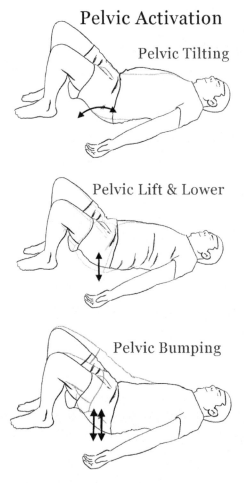

Pelvic Activation

Pelvic Tilting

Pelvic Lift & Lower

Pelvic Bumping

This series of three exercises, done lying down on a mat, flow nicely into one other and serve to progressively wake up the pelvic area. I say "wake up" because actually this part of our body in many ways has its own mind. It knows intuitively how to move the body in order to free it from the influences of cortical inhibition, or repression. But this capacity for self-healing has been held in check by our higher mind, culturally suppressed because the pelvic area is also the seat of our sexuality. In Western culture we simply don't allow our pelvic to move naturally, for fear of appearing overly sexual. We tend to restrict sexuality to the image-making and thinking capacity of our minds.

Lying down on a mat in the Reichian Working Position, first spend a few minutes Belly Breathing. Then we move into the first of our pelvic exercises. It involves 'rolling' the pelvis – tilting it forwards and back using the tailbone as a fulcrum. Inhaling, we tilt our pelvis down, lifting our lower back off the mat and taking our ass down towards it. Exhaling, reverse this movement, bringing the lower back flat on the mat and the ass up. Continue following the breath in this manner for 10 minutes, tilting your pelvis to the max but at no time allowing your tailbone to come off the mat. Ideally, keep your eyes closed throughout this whole sequence of exercises and remain feeling deeply into the pelvic area. But if you find yourself drifting off excessively, then I recommend you open your eyes and focus on a point on the ceiling above you.

After 10 minutes of the first exercise, we move into the second. This is called the 'Pelvic Lift & Lower.' Inhaling, slowly lift your tailbone about two inches (5 cms) off the mat. Exhaling, gently bring it down again. Lift and lower the pelvis gently and really feel each nuance of the movement. This is important. Do not lift it more than two inches. It is a feeling exercise rather than a big physical lift. Continue for 10 minutes.

After 10 minutes of the second exercise, we transition into an exercise known as 'Pelvic Bumping.' It is identical to 'Pelvic Lift & Lower' but for one small change. On the exhale, instead of gently lowering the tailbone back to the mat, simply let it drop without controlling its descent in any way. So, inhaling gently lift the tailbone two inches. Exhaling, simply let it drop back to the mat. You should feel a characteristic bump as it hits the mat. This should not be painful. If it is, you may need to double the thickness of the mat. Whilst bumping your tailbone in this manner, continue to really feel into your pelvis. You may discover, at some point, that your pelvis begins to bump up and down seemingly of its own accord and at its own rate. This can be disturbing for the mind but it is actually very healthy. So, if it begins to happen, try to simply allow your pelvis to do its thing.

Perform this final exercise for between ten and thirty minutes and then bring this sequence to a close by lying flat out on the mat relaxing for five to ten minutes.

Pelvic Floor Opening Sequence

Pelvic Floor Opening Sequence

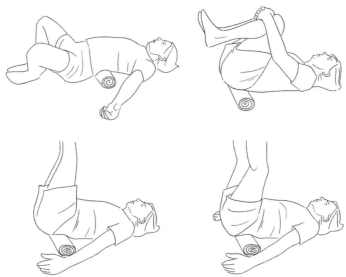

This nifty series of four exercises is great for opening the pelvic floor and helping to keep it open. Getting this area of our body more open helps us to ground and reduces neediness. We don't need to cling to others when energy can flow down through our bodies and out to the earth. I recommend using a 60 second ding when doing this sequence and completing three reps.

Lying on your back on a yoga mat, bring the soles of your feet together with your knees wide. This posture is known as the Diamond Leg Posture in yoga. Use a second, rolled-up yoga mat as a bolster and place it under your lower back.

At the ding, come into the second posture, the Reverse Lower Back Stretch. First, lift your ass so that you can move your bolster to under your tailbone. Then bring your knees toward your chest, clasping them with your arms. Try to keep your knees and ankles touching whilst doing this.

At the ding, keeping the bolster under your tailbone, release your knees and bring your legs up into a Classic Leg Stretch. Endeavour to straighten both legs fully through the knees and to keep them at ninety degrees to the trunk of the body.

At the ding, keeping your legs straight through the knees and at ninety degrees to the trunk of the body, spread your legs wide into a 'Y' shape. Leave the bolster under your tailbone.

When the ding sounds, relax your legs for a moment and come back into the Diamond Leg Posture, moving the bolster back to under your lower back. Begin your second set.

Push Breathing

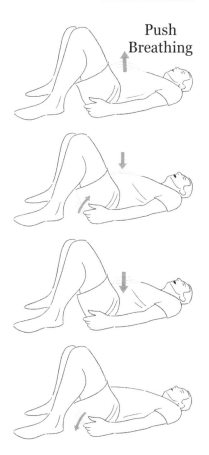

Push
Breathing

This slightly modified Reichian exercise is an excellent example of the way that breathing techniques can be combined with body movements to release the past. Like the exercises above, it works especially with the pelvic area. It is done in the Reichian Working Position explained at the beginning of this chapter and has four elements to it. I will list them separately, to hopefully make it clearer:

1) Perform an inhale by inflating your belly, just as you would when practising Belly Breathing.

2) When your inhale is complete, begin to exhale by relaxing your belly and making a gentle "Ah" sound. As you do this, slowly tilt your pelvis towards your head, such that your lower back comes flat on the mat.

3) When you have exhaled all that you can by gently relaxing your belly, keeping your pelvis tilted up, compress your belly back into the abdominal cavity, pushing out any remaining air.

4) When fully exhaled, without beginning the next inhale, slowly tilt your pelvis back to the start position. Begin the next inhale as above and repeat the sequence.

This is most definitely a tricky technique to get the hang of. Take it slowly to begin with, making sure you have really got each stage. When you are confident with it, feel free to practise it, perhaps with some gentle music, for 30 minutes or more.

Rapid Inhale Belly Breathing

This highly evocative exercise, developed by Wilhelm Reich, both rapidly increases the charge of energy in the core of the body and supports us to feel our belly area more.

Before attempting the exercise, you do need to feel confident with regular Belly Breathing, explained earlier on in the chapter. That's to say, you need to be able to breathe solely by extending and relaxing your abdominal muscles, whilst your chest remains unmoving, your throat and neck muscles are relaxed and your breath is soundless.

Lying down on a yoga mat in the Reichian Working Position, first spend some minutes performing Belly Breathing. When ready, begin to achieve the inhale by flicking your abdominals quickly up and holding them there for a second or two. The flick should take between a quarter and a half of a second and should create a full inhale. It should also be pretty much soundless. After you've held your abs fully out for a couple of seconds, begin a normal Belly Breathing exhale, slowly relaxing your abs and slightly contracting them. I recommend doing the exhale with a relaxed "Ah" sound. Once exhaled, begin the next inhale with the flicking technique again and continue.

So, to sum up, the exhale is identical to that of regular Belly Breathing. But the inhale is done with a flick of the abs which is then held for a second or two. I recommend practising this technique for 5 minutes at a time initially. It's quite normal to feel yourself becoming breathless to begin with. This is because the throat is still not adequately relaxed. To practise, it may be easier to alternate the inhales between flicking the abs and slowly extending them, as in normal Belly Breathing, one after the other.

Right-to-Exist Exercise

This excellent Bioenergetic exercise really does the job of getting your belly active. It's my favourite exercise for people working with their Oral or Endurer sides.

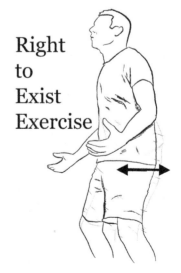

Right to Exist Exercise

The Right-to-Exist Exercise is an excellent example of how using a specific body movement can create a psychological shift. The primal movement of self-assertion that it encapsulates will progressively create a psychological shift within you.

Over time, it will give you more confidence in stating your needs and moving towards getting them met.

Stand upright with your feet wider than shoulder-width apart, your knees bent and the outsides of your feet roughly parallel. Your backbone should be upright, and you should feel flexible on the vertical axis, such that you could bounce your ass up and down if you wished.

Pull your hips slightly back and then thrust them forwards, with assertiveness, whilst making a distinct, low grunt sound. The grunt should be the lowest sound you can make. Your backbone should remain upright throughout, and the movement should only be from the hips to the knees. Your arms should be by your side, or slightly forwards, with your palms open and facing front, as though you were about to receive something.

Reinforce the effect of this exercise by putting an atavistic, animal look on your face and allowing yourself to embody the sense that "I just wanna get something!" Get into the raw sensation of this and allow it to show in each thrust of your pelvis.

Do this exercise initially for 5 minutes, at a rate of roughly one thrust per second. Build up to 20 minutes over time. I recommend you use a 'grunt track' to keep time. You can download one from the website mentioned in the Resources section at the end of this book.

Shoulder Opening Sequence

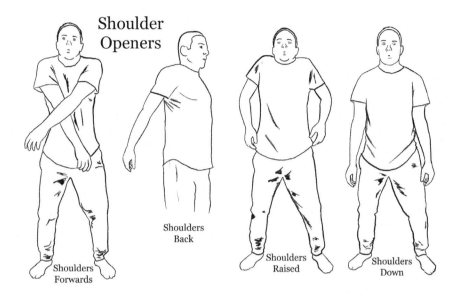

Shoulder Openers

Shoulders Forwards

Shoulders Back

Shoulders Raised

Shoulders Down

This series of exercises, that run together, is another foundational practice from Bioenergetics. Do them regularly and you will most definitely notice a shift in your levels of shoulder tension and how open your chest feels. If you have physical issues with one or both shoulders, I recommend checking in first with your physician before doing them. They can be helpful for conditions like a 'frozen shoulder' but it's important to check in first.

Beginning from the Grounded Standing Stance (see beginning of chapter), we are going to run through a series of four static shoulder stretches that are each held for a time between 1 and 2 minutes. Each stretch should be completed by throwing the arms and shoulders downward with a grunt sound. At no time should you use your arms as levers, to increase the stretch. Simply allow your arms and hands to be relaxed. The stretch is in the shoulders only.

Stretch #1 – Pull your shoulders forwards, as though trying to get them to touch in the front of your chest. Keep applying forward pressure as you breathe with your belly and feel your body.

Stretch #2 – Pull your shoulders back, as though trying to get your shoulder blades to touch. Perhaps imagine you have a walnut between your shoulder blades that you are trying to crack. Again, keep applying pressure whilst belly breathing and feeling your body.

Stretch #3 – Pull your shoulders up towards your ears, as high as you can. This stretch is the most energetically evocative and most people slacken off within a few seconds. I recommend that you practice it in front of a mirror to check you're maintaining it. Breathe and feel throughout as before.

Stretch #4 – Pull your shoulders down, as though carrying heavy weights. This stretch is usually the easiest but still give it your all, breathing and feeling throughout.

I recommend you perform 3 reps of this sequence to get the maximum effect. Begin with a 1 minute ding and feel free to increase this up to 2 minutes if beneficial.

Shoulders Raise

I listed this exercise directly above in the Shoulder Opening Sequence. But it is so evocative that it is also really worth doing on its own, or fitting it into other sequences.

From the Grounded Standing Stance, simply lift your shoulders towards your ears, as high as you can get them. Your arms should be relaxed. You may find that they naturally bend at the elbows but this is fine as long as you're not exerting any control over them. Your hands and fingers should also be loose.

Endeavour to keep pulling your shoulders up higher, maintaining that pressure until the exercise is over. This stretch is so evocative that, in my experience, most people will slacken off after a few seconds. So, stay present! Also, check that your knees remain at least slightly bent and certainly not locked straight. Locking the knees when standing is a way to keep deeper feelings down.

It's very important to keep Belly Breathing and feeling your body throughout. Begin practising this stretch for 1 minute and work up to 5 minutes as you get used to it.

Somatic Centre Sensing

In the way that I teach Bioenergetics, what we are primarily working with is the sense of the body. We are learning to increase the amount that we can feel it and this is intrinsically healing. This simple meditative exercise is excellent to really get this. I recommend doing it on a 1 to 2 minute ding and performing two or three reps.

Sitting or kneeling, with eyes open or closed, simply feel into the area of your perineum – between your anus and genitals. It's important not to make any sound, or visualise anything. This is solely a feeling exercise. Look for any sensation in that area that you can 'anchor' your awareness to. If you don't find any, keep trying. It is the action of trying to feel that creates change.

At the ding, move up to the area of your belly, inside your body cavity, and continue. Next move to the solar plexus area. Then the centre of your chest. Then your throat. Then inside the centre of your head. Finally, shift your awareness to the very top of your head.

Note that, aside from the first and last areas, which are on the surface of the body, for the other five areas, you try to feel into the body at that point.

Spinal Feeling Journey Exercise

This exercise is very similar to the previous one, Somatic Centre Sensing. However, this time we will focus solely on feeling into different areas of the spine. This will help us to feel our back more. If we don't feel our back sufficiently, then we will tend to either cling on to others, for support, or to keep everything under very tight control at a mental level, neither of which are great options!

I recommend using a 1-minute ding track for this exercise and completing two or three reps. Remember, it's all about tuning in purely to the sense of the body. Do your best not to be distracted by thinking and do not use tones or visual imagery in any way.

Sitting or kneeling comfortably, with eyes closed, begin to feel into the area of your tailbone. Focus solely, but without creating tension, on the sense of your body in this area. At the ding, consciously move your awareness up your spine to your lower back area and continue feeling. Then to the mid-back, followed by the area between the shoulder-blades. Continue, at the ding, to the midpoint of your neck and finally to the occipital point, the point of your head furthest back.

Sucking Gesture Exercise

The reflex to suck becomes available to us as soon as we are born. It is only with us for our first few years, making this very useful for body-based therapy. When we re-learn the sucking gesture as adults, our psychological state slowly returns to early infancy, and this

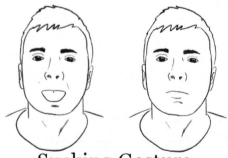

Sucking Gesture

can allow all sorts of issues that arrived later to be released. It takes a little practice. But once you've got it, the exercise is easy. However, like the eye movement exercises, despite being quite easy and not so physical, a lot of deep emotion and buried energy can be activated. So do take care of yourself and practice self-awareness for the rest of the day after doing a sucking gesture exercise.

I recommend first practising the sucking gesture whilst sitting down comfortably. Stick your tongue most of the way out and, if you can, bring it down towards your chin. Now, in one quick movement, suck it back in through gently closed lips such that it makes a "tpp" sound. Slightly open your mouth, stick your tongue out again and repeat. You can kind of feel when you've got it right. Otherwise look for the video on my YouTube channel to see a demo.

Once you've got the hang of the exercise, you are ready to perform it lying down, in the Reichian Working Position. Have your eyes closed, perform the sucking gesture and remain tuned in to the sense of the body. To reinforce the potency of the exercise, you can try contracting your sphincter muscles as you suck your tongue back in and relaxing them as it comes back out.

I recommend that you perform this exercise for 10 minutes to begin with and work up to one hour.

Teenager Release

Our teenage years, whilst a drag for many parents, are very important psychologically. It's the time that we begin to throw off the influence of our parents. Teenagers spontaneously begin to make a specific shrugging movement to achieve this, though its psychological significance is usually not recognised. Rather it just feels good.

In the Grounded Standing Stance, lift your shoulders towards your ears and in one quick movement throw them down hard with a slightly grouchy grunting sound, like you're not happy about something. Your knees should not be locked straight when you do this. Do one throw-down every few seconds.

Teenager Release

You can do the exercise standing still but it also works well to do it walking around. Perhaps imagine that you are a teenager again, and that one of your parents is giving you a big lecture about something. You know you have to comply, but you want to show them that you're not happy about it, hence you throw your shoulders down with a grunt.

When practised at this, you can escalate it to throwing your shoulders down more rapidly, perhaps five times within one breath, and making a continuous sound of annoyance.

This exercise is excellent for accessing repressed anger, when done over time.

Trust Fall Exercise

This exercise will require a small group of people, at least 4 or 5. You form a tight circle, standing up, and one person goes in the middle and closes their eyes. They gently allow themselves to sway to the point where they begin to fall. Right at that moment, the group stops them from actually falling with their hands. As a supporter, you must allow the person in the middle to experience letting go of control and just starting to fall but obviously you quickly stop them from actually falling.

The person in the middle should experience falling and being caught several times, then stand and feel their body for around 15–30 seconds. Someone else can then take their place.

Additional Writings

Have Changes in Society Affected Character Structure?

Reich's original work, Character Analysis, was first published in the early 1930s, nearly a century ago. Since then, Western society, in particular, has been on a huge journey. Another world war, mutually-assured-destruction, flower-power, the internet, climate change and more have all taken place. The pressure on our culture for social change has been immense.

With regards to Character Structure, by far the most prominent area of change has been in how we typically bring up children. The overtly harsh, repressive regimes of Reich's time have been gradually displaced by gentler, more caring parenting. This has inevitably altered how Character Structure manifests in today's world. Not so much in the actual Types; they remain the same. But rather in the reduced tendency for today's generation to manifest simply one or two dominant Structures. For the twenty and thirty-somethings of the 2020s, all of the Character Structures are more likely to be evident, in varying degrees, in each person.

Another factor here may be the reality that people are more 'in their minds' these days. More and more of us interact with the world through an online presence, or avatar. This lack of physicality enables even those most locked into, say, the Leaving Structure, to act as though they are Rigid or Aggressive.

As mentioned in an earlier chapter, we are also more sensitive and more likely to apply a DIY approach to facing psychological issues these days. This has created a need to re-interpret Character Structure in both more practical and less pathologising language.

These things have led me to reformulate Character Analysis, the result of which is this book. Moving away from pathologising and technical psychiatric language to the more accessible and friendly notions of Safety Strategies can potentially provide a launchpad for a renaissance in Character Structure. In my experience, pretty much anyone can relate to the three pre-egoic Safety Strategies and find benefit in them, regardless of whether they appear to tie precisely to their own personal childhood or body shape.

The clingy feeling of the Oral Type, the spacey feeling of the Leaving, or the self-undermining tendencies of the Endurer - just by being able to categorise and understand these behaviours is, of itself, just so healing. We say "Ah, I get it now!"

I hope this book can inspire others to expand and continue the work of Character Structure.

Psychosis as an Extension of the Leaving Structure

One of the unfortunate things about Reichian Character Structure is that, as it has become progressively marginalised over the years, the benefit of learning about it has also been diminished. Where is the reward? What will it give me to learn all this stuff? Reasonable questions, I think.

However, one of the clear benefits that I see is the opportunity to demystify many aspects of mental health. Psychiatry is something of a closed shop. To get through the door, you need to undertake years of study with an approved organisation. If and when you do finally enter into its hallowed grounds, do you now have the tools to understand day-to-day mental health issues with ease? Not really, in my opinion.

Unfortunately, being a psychiatrist, or having a PhD in clinical psychology, does not give you so much really practical, useful knowledge. It gives you access to lots of modern, and invariably complex-sounding theories, about depression, anxiety and more. But it doesn't give you a simple and effective model for understanding these conditions.

Reichian Character Structure makes a great deal more progress here. Understanding how the Oral Character is formed we begin to develop a useful model for mapping out why some people seem so prone to depression or addiction. Understanding that dissociation from the body can take place – the Leaving Structure – allows us to usefully see how this can easily lead to anxiety.

It's not hard science. You cannot prove it. But the models provided do make sense on multiple levels, and, furthermore, point towards treatment directions. They also allow people suffering from these conditions to make sense of them, to track them back to safety strategies that were needed early in life. As anyone who has suffered, without any understanding as to why or of what needs to happen knows, this is no small thing.

Nowhere is this more apparent than in trying to understand psychosis. Psychosis is a significant mental health condition where an individual appears to lose all contact with reality. Their behaviour and thinking become significantly different from others. They may appear to see phenomena that we don't. They may be attributing a significance to events or people that we would not. Sometimes there appears to be a 'trigger' for the onset of the condition. Sometimes it appears to be more cyclical, coming and going according to some hidden, perhaps neurobiological factor.

Witnessing someone you know having a 'psychotic episode' can be terrifying. In a small number of instances they can even be dangerous to themselves or others. But what is really going on? Is there a simple model we can use to understand psychosis and support someone suffering from it? Yes, there is.

Psychosis is an extension of the Leaving Pattern. If, during the beginning of our development, we learned to dissociate from the feeling of the body and reside in the safer environs of the mind, we will have become familiar with the notion of abstract worlds.

Many healthy children go through a phase where they attribute labels or qualities to things around them that we would not strictly consider accurate. Perhaps a favourite cuddly toy acquires a name and a personality. Perhaps a teacher at school is seen as an ogre or witch. Perhaps parents acquire the names of characters in a TV series.

This behaviour, for some, continues into adulthood. The mind, when idle, creates these fantasy worlds where perhaps the individual themselves has more importance than they usually experience out in the world. In these worlds, those around them take on archetypal roles – the evil witch, the good son, the despotic father, the beautiful princess, and so on.

Although this behaviour can be a way to avoid feelings of low self-esteem, there is not necessarily so much wrong with it. It is rather as though one has found a 'trapdoor' in the ceiling and learned to pass through it into a world where we have much more control over what goes on. It's a world where all the usual reference points have a different significance.

What makes this behaviour not especially unhealthy is that we can come back down. We can come out of our own private world and back into the consensual social reality that we share with others.

Psychosis is when you can't or won't come back down. It's when you remain in your abstract world and can't seem to find a way back to the day-to-day reality where people, objects and events have an agreed meaning. Despite finding yourself in social situations where it's incumbent on you to 'behave normally,' you either can't or won't do it. You continue to behave as though you are in the abstract world you have created in your mind. This inevitably causes people to talk and at some point, if you remain this dissociated, likely the psychiatric authorities will be called in.

The key to understanding psychosis in this model is to recognise that this inability, or at times refusal, to return to the normal world is the result of some level of emotional triggering. We have this 'escape route' already mapped out in our mind. Something happens in our world, or an organic process in the brain has begun, and we flee up through our trapdoor to escape.

What is needed is a feeling of safety. When our nervous system truly registers that things are now safe for us, we will begin to return to the normal world. This can happen through whatever triggered our flight from reality coming to a close. Or it can simply be that a cyclical brain process that predisposed us to this behaviour comes to a conclusion and enters a different phase.

I have found that looking at psychosis this way has been very helpful. It can give those who have suffered it a simple means to understand the condition and to plan out how not to return to it. It can help those who care about someone to know what to do to be of support.

Addiction as an Extension of the Oral Structure

Another example of a common mental health condition that can be usefully modelled through the lens of Character Structure is addiction. Whatever the substance or behaviour that proves addictive, invariably there will be an aspect where there is a sense of trying to fill 'an inner hole.' There is an underlying neediness, often not even registered consciously, but lurking there beneath the surface and regularly motivating addictive behaviours.

This is clearly the result of the Oral side of our character. Not getting the connection with the mother that we expected and needed in our very early infancy has created this sense of lack within – a hole which, try as we might, never seems to get filled, at least not for any meaningful length of time.

Whether we rely on alcohol, drugs, shopping, or ritual behaviours as our addiction, there is this inner neediness, this sense that we need something to take us away from what is going on inside. We are not okay as we are.

I must be honest here and state that I don't consider the connection between the Oral side of our nature and addiction to be quite so straightforward as that between psychosis and the Leaving Structure. The motivation for certain addictive behaviours can also come from the Enduring or Rigid sides of our personalities. It seems to me that addictive tendencies also relate to how we learn to derive pleasure from life whilst in a state of at least partial dissociation from the body.

Resources

My YouTube Channel - https://www.youtube.com/c/DevarajSandberg

My Website - https://bioenergetics.org.uk/

Ding Track downloads - https://www.bioenergetics.org.uk/downloads/

Recommended Further Reading - The 5 Personality Patterns by Steven Kessler

Printed in Great Britain
by Amazon

39716302R00106